# Understanding
# DOLLS

## Caroline G. Goodfellow

Antique Collectors' Club

© 1983 Antique Collectors' Club
World copyright reserved
Paperback edition 1986
ISBN 1 85149 006 X

British Library CIP Data
Goodfellow, Caroline
Understanding Dolls
1. Dolls — Collectors and collecting
I. Title
745.592'21     NK4893

Published for the Antique Collectors' Club by the
Antique Collectors' Club Ltd.

Printed in England by the Antique Collectors' Club Ltd.,
Woodbridge, Suffolk.

*Frontispiece. Two English dolls, carved and painted wood with glass eyes; head and torso type. Right: 1700-20, height 19ins. Left: known as Sophie, c.1760, height 24¾ins.*

# Antique Collectors' Club

The Antique Collectors' Club was formed in 1966 and now has a five figure membership spread throughout the world. It publishes the only independently run monthly antiques magazine *Antique Collecting* which caters for those collectors who are interested in widening their knowledge of antiques, both by greater awareness of quality and by discussion of the factors which influence the price that is likely to be asked. The Antique Collectors' Club pioneered the provision of information on prices for collectors and the magazine still leads in the provision of detailed articles on a variety of subjects.

It was in response to the enormous demand for information on "what to pay" that the price guide series was introduced in 1968 with the first edition of *The Price Guide to Antique Furniture* (completely revised, 1978), a book which broke new ground by illustrating the more common types of antique furniture, the sort that collectors could buy in shops and at auctions rather than the rare museum pieces which had previously been used (and still to a large extent are used) to make up the limited amount of illustrations in books published by commercial publishers. Many other price guides have followed, all copiously illustrated, and greatly appreciated by collectors for the valuable information they contain, quite apart from prices. The Antique Collectors' Club also publishes other books on antiques, including horology and art reference works, and a full book list is available.

Club membership, which is open to all collectors, costs £12.95 per annum. Members receive free of charge *Antique Collecting,* the Club's magazine (published every month except August), which contains well-illustrated articles dealing with the practical aspects of collecting not normally dealt with by magazines. Prices, features of value, investment potential, fakes and forgeries are all given prominence in the magazine.

Among other facilities available to members are private buying and selling facilities, the longest list of "For Sales" of any antiques magazine, an annual ceramics conference and the opportunity to meet other collectors at their local antique collectors' clubs. There are nearly eighty in Britain and so far a dozen overseas. Members may also buy the Club's publications at special pre-publication prices.

As its motto implies, the Club is an amateur organisation designed to help collectors get the most out of their hobby: it is informal and friendly and gives enormous enjoyment to all concerned.

*For Collectors — By Collectors — About Collecting*

**The Antique Collectors' Club**
**5 Church Street, Woodbridge, Suffolk**

# Acknowledgements

All the dolls illustrated are in the collection housed by Bethnal Green Museum of Childhood, London, which holds the Crown Copyright.

I would like to express my thanks for the invaluable assistance of Elizabeth Aslin and Faith Eaton, and the staff of Bethnal Green Museum of Childhood for their help and unfailing support.

PHOTOGRAPHY BY KEN JACKSON.

# Contents

# Colour Plates

# Introduction

The dolls discussed and illustrated in this book are drawn from the collection housed in the Bethnal Green Museum of Childhood. The collection, numbering several thousands, covers the wide range of dolls made by children and parents, and by crafts and mass-production, over a three hundred year period. The aim of the collection is to present a history of dolls and to this end, the collection is constantly being added to. The aims differ from those of the private collector in that there are no huge stocks of dolls by one maker or of one particular type, but as wide a variety as is possible.

As the doll collector within the museum, I try to exercise an unbiased attitude to all the dolls and to reflect the development of an industry. All dolls should be equal whether they are cheap or expensive, beautiful or ugly, old or new. Thousands of dolls pass through my hands each year and I know that at some time in their history a person has owned, enjoyed and even loved their doll. Even dolls which have been found in attics or dug up in gardens have commanded enough respect from their finder for the person to bring them to me with the one question, "Please tell me all about it."

This book, prompted by this question, should allow you to understand your doll, its history and manufacture and thus to increase your enjoyment of it.

Not everyone is fortunate enough to have a 17th or 18th century wooden doll, indeed not everyone actually likes them, but you may find one day a strangely shaped lump of wood. Would you be able to distinguish it from the top of a newel post? On the other hand you may dig up a white ceramic head, realise that it is a doll's head, but wonder why it has no colour. Unless you have a doll which has a known history or one with a convenient, easily read mark upon it, it is not usually possible to know who made it, where it was made or its approximate age, without seeking assistance. This book has been devised to assist you to do personal research and it will give you the basis of an overall picture of your doll. You will learn of its origins and date, and possibly of its maker.

A doll is made from a number of features which have changed

over the years to adapt the doll for new looks, styles and uses. The most obvious changes are those to the materials used for its construction, followed closely by the changes to its head. Each chapter will deal with a different feature. The index includes the period over which particular dolls were made.

Dolls are quite fragile and many are breakable. Set out on pp. 12 and 13 is a chart for you to copy. Initially study your doll, feature by feature, and fill the chart in with the details. You will be able to discover some of the features just by looking at the doll, for example whether the eyes close or if the mouth is open showing teeth. Other features you may have a guess at, such as the type of hair used for the wig. Some features, however, you may not know at all, such as what material was used to make the limbs. The purpose of filling out the chart is to allow you to read the book without constantly handling the doll.

Often quoted is "My doll has a china head with a body made of a different substance." The chart is a set of guideline questions to assist in establishing the basic details of a doll and armed with the answers you can then study the information given in this book and seek further help if needed. The index can be followed to give you an idea when all the features of your doll match in date, thus establishing the approximate date of manufacture.

## Using Reference Books and Museums and Libraries

Having gained the initial knowledge from this book, you may feel you need to do further research. Your first step is to consult your local library. Most libraries carry a few books on dolls but not all may have the larger books such as *The Collectors' Encyclopaedia of Dolls*. These, however, may be borrowed through the library's loan services. You may, on the other hand, decide to buy the books. This is a good idea if you plan to increase your collection of dolls.

Your local museum should also be able to help you, though probably with the suggestion to seek advice from a museum specialising in dolls (a list of museums is given on p. 232). It is not wise to take your doll to a museum on the off chance that someone can help you. Check first that someone will be able to help, make an appointment to see them and pack your doll for the journey very carefully. Such arrangements will save time, disappointment, and worry over the doll's safety.

If you are unable to visit a specialist museum, write to the museum with all the details you know about your doll, possibly enclosing a copy of your chart. Send recognisable photographs or drawings showing the head and body of the doll. No one expects professional photographs, but a tiny figure sat in a large chair, which is taken out of focus, really does not assist the person trying to help you identify your doll. Always remember, the more detail you provide the more information becomes available to the specialist and in turn to you. Occasionally you may be asked to bring the doll in question to the museum because a point arises which cannot be seen or decided upon by looking at a photograph.

Museums and libraries are usually good sources to go to for information about other collections, clubs, etc. Make use of them.

Reference books can be extremely complicated to use but once mastered extremely useful. If we use the mark example shown in Plate 151 (p. 185) and consult *The Collectors' Encyclopaedia of Dolls,* here are guidelines to follow. The book itself is laid out in alphabetical order and includes doll types, makers, trademarks and names. Our maker conveniently has a listing under Marseille, Armand in the text. However, the general index lists the pages and photograph numbers where the name appears throughout the text. Additionally there is a numerical index showing where 390 occurs and an initial and abbreviation index showing AM. There are other indexes covering details which may appear on a doll or its box, such as a date, an address, letters (with or without a number), names, words and phrases, and symbols and shapes. Anyone of these will lead you to a possible answer.

By reading the text, studying the photographs and checking all the cross references, you will gain a lot of information about the maker and his work, and the doll itself, and how it relates to other dolls made at the same time. Photographs are usually more revealing than the text as the latter is quite brief, but of course, not every example of a maker's product nor his marks can be shown and it is possible that you will not find a duplicate of your doll or its mark. On the other hand, if you cannot trace your doll through the indexes, by glancing at the photographs you may come across one which is similar in style to yours and thus set the pattern for the information you need.

11

# Doll Collectors' Chart

*HEAD*
1. Shape or type . . . . . . . . . . . . . . . . . . . . . . . . . . . . . . . . . . . . . . . . . . . . . . . .
2. Material . . . . . . . . . . . . . . . . . . . . . . . . . . . . . . . . . . . . . . . . . . . . . . . . . . .

*BODY*
1. Shape . . . . . . . . . . . . . . . . . . . . . . . . . . . . . . . . . . . . . . . . . . . . . . . . . . . .
2. Material . . . . . . . . . . . . . . . . . . . . . . . . . . . . . . . . . . . . . . . . . . . . . . . . . .
3. Jointing . . . . . . . . . . . . . . . . . . . . . . . . . . . . . . . . . . . . . . . . . . . . . . . . . .

*ARMS*
1. Type . . . . . . . . . . . . . . . . . . . . . . . . . . . . . . . . . . . . . . . . . . . . . . . . . . . . .
2. Upper . . . . . . . . . . . . . . . . . . . . . . . . . . . . . . . . . . . . . . . . . . . . . . . . . . . .
3. Lower . . . . . . . . . . . . . . . . . . . . . . . . . . . . . . . . . . . . . . . . . . . . . . . . . . . .
4. Hands . . . . . . . . . . . . . . . . . . . . . . . . . . . . . . . . . . . . . . . . . . . . . . . . . . . .
5. Material . . . . . . . . . . . . . . . . . . . . . . . . . . . . . . . . . . . . . . . . . . . . . . . . . .
6. Jointing . . . . . . . . . . . . . . . . . . . . . . . . . . . . . . . . . . . . . . . . . . . . . . . . . .

*LEGS*
1. Type . . . . . . . . . . . . . . . . . . . . . . . . . . . . . . . . . . . . . . . . . . . . . . . . . . . . .
2. Upper . . . . . . . . . . . . . . . . . . . . . . . . . . . . . . . . . . . . . . . . . . . . . . . . . . . .
3. Lower . . . . . . . . . . . . . . . . . . . . . . . . . . . . . . . . . . . . . . . . . . . . . . . . . . . .
4. Feet . . . . . . . . . . . . . . . . . . . . . . . . . . . . . . . . . . . . . . . . . . . . . . . . . . . . .
5. Material . . . . . . . . . . . . . . . . . . . . . . . . . . . . . . . . . . . . . . . . . . . . . . . . . .
6. Jointing . . . . . . . . . . . . . . . . . . . . . . . . . . . . . . . . . . . . . . . . . . . . . . . . . .

*FACE*
1. Shape . . . . . . . . . . . . . . . . . . . . . . . . . . . . . . . . . . . . . . . . . . . . . . . . . . . .
2. Material . . . . . . . . . . . . . . . . . . . . . . . . . . . . . . . . . . . . . . . . . . . . . . . . . .
3. Colouring . . . . . . . . . . . . . . . . . . . . . . . . . . . . . . . . . . . . . . . . . . . . . . . . .
4. Features, nose, dimples, ears . . . . . . . . . . . . . . . . . . . . . . . . . . . . . . . . . . .
5. Mouth type . . . . . . . . . . . . . . . . . . . . . . . . . . . . . . . . . . . . . . . . . . . . . . . .

*EYES*
1. Type . . . . . . . . . . . . . . . . . . . . . . . . . . . . . . . . . . . . . . . . . . . . . . . . . . . . .
2. Material . . . . . . . . . . . . . . . . . . . . . . . . . . . . . . . . . . . . . . . . . . . . . . . . . .
3. Type of movement . . . . . . . . . . . . . . . . . . . . . . . . . . . . . . . . . . . . . . . . . . .

*HAIR*
1. Type ......................................................
2. Material ..................................................
3. Method of Affixing ......................................

*MARKS AND LABELS*
Draw any marks or labels as
carefully as possible and
note where they occur on
the doll (e.g. shoulder).
Decide whether the marks
are stamped or incised. ....................................

*ODDITIES*
If the doll is possibly a 'character'
1. Describe expression .....................................
2. Give known name (for example historical character (e.g. Lord
Roberts), manufacturer's name (e.g. My Dream Baby) or family name
(e.g. Sophie) ..............................................

*MECHANICAL DOLLS*
1. Type of movement .......................................
2. Control or mechanism ...................................

*AGE*
1. Assess on known history .................................
2. Record any information known about doll .................
3. Check clothing ..........................................

*SIZE*
1. Overall height ...........................................
2. Height of head ..........................................
3. Circumference of head ...................................

*DAMAGE*
1. Note damage or wear to both head and body ..............
2. Damage to clothing ......................................

# Chapter 1
## The Heads

The most prominent part of a doll and the item to first decide upon is the type of head which has been used to construct your doll. The type, when considered by itself, will give an indication of the date of the doll. When considered in conjunction with other characteristics such as the material, facial features and body, the head will give a fairly accurate date.

Some head designs lasted for many years, such as the head and torso combination, while others did not begin until quite late and lasted only a short time, such as the swivel neck. It must always be remembered that a doll need not be as old as the earliest date given in this book or that found in other reference books. Any date depends on the doll as a whole unit rather than on one characteristic. However, it is safe to assume (unless you have had the misfortune to have acquired a fake) that the doll was not made after the last known date of the type, manufacture or its maker.

There may be occasions when you will have a doll with a replacement part, for example the head or a part of the body. You should be able to discover this fact if you follow through the methods and steps of identification. There is nothing wrong with a doll which has a replacement; it just means that at sometime in its history, it has had a bad accident.

When you examine your doll's head you may find one odd and possibly disturbing feature — its size. A doll's head is proportionally larger compared with the rest of the body than a human head. In some cases, the differences between the length of the face and the size of the hands and feet are very noticeable but in no way are they unusual for a doll. In extreme cases, some makers while trying to create the illusion of an expensive doll created very disproportionate heads and bodies. These dolls had large heads on long over-stuffed cloth bodies with short rather fat lower arms and legs which were generally made of a ceramic material.

# All-in-One Dolls

The simplest construction for making a doll is to create it as a single unit without limbs. This is the principle used for dolls which normally represent babies in swaddling clothes. Usually made of wood, these dolls were crudely hewn and painted and did little but rest in a cradle or in the arms of their owners. The common name for them now is POUPARD.

The doll shown in Plate 1 is of carved wood, with the nose made of a triangle of wood placed into a slit in the face. It is painted in blue, red, pink and yellow and stands 11ins. tall. On its back is written "Schnattifino der Rupel. Geborenze Sterzing 20 Juli 1926" — Schnattifino, the awkward one born Sterzing July 20, 1926. Representing a boy, it is one of a pair and the other, representing a girl, is similarly inscribed but with the name and title "Thymiane die Dufrende" — Thymiane, the aromatic one. Plate 133 (p. 165) shows the slit for the nose. The majority of this type of doll were made in Erzgebirge, an area of Saxony near the Bohemian border. This Poupard is the simplest design of a whole family of wooden dolls produced in Europe for over 300 years. Many were lathe-turned with separate arms and legs rather than carved and, when used in conjunction with other pieces, formed toys such as Noah's Arks, farm and village sets and even groups of soldiers.

As more sophisticated casting methods were used, dolls with limbs were produced. Called by a range of names such as Bathing Babies, Frozen Charlottes, Pillar Dolls, and Solid Chinas, these dolls had rigid limbs formed with the body. They were introduced during the mid-19th century and their most common features were clenched fists and standing four-square on their feet. Generally of glazed china, either white or tinted pink, they had moulded hair styles and facial features. Production of these dolls continued until about 1910 and they ranged in size from 1in. to 18ins.

The example shown in Plate 2 has a white glazed china body with black hair and it stands 10ins. tall. In common with most of this type of doll, it was made in Germany.

Occasionally, one may find a wax or celluloid All-in-One doll. However, wax is a fragile material and the dolls found in this material tend to be small and housed in a cradle. An example is shown in Plate 3. It is a wax figure with painted features and hair,

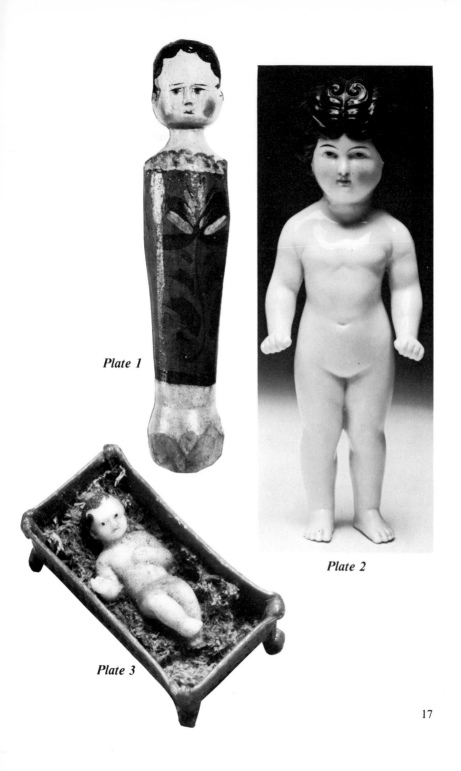

*Plate 1*

*Plate 2*

*Plate 3*

representing a baby. It is lying in a cradle made of celluloid on a bed of dried foliage. The doll is 1⅜ins. long and the cradle 2ins.

A variation of the completely rigid figure was developed where the arms were separate and joined to each other through the rigid head, torso and legs. This allowed slight movement. Later dolls made of china or bisque were produced where the limbs were added to a head and torso. These are not classified as All-in-One dolls and they follow the dictates set by the dolls with moving limbs.

The KEWPIE, all bisque figure shown in Plate 4 is jointed only at the shoulders, with painted features and intaglio eyes. The Kewpie Doll was designed by an American called Rose O'Neill and this example was probably made by J.D. Kestner of Waltershausen in about 1913. It stands 5ins. tall.

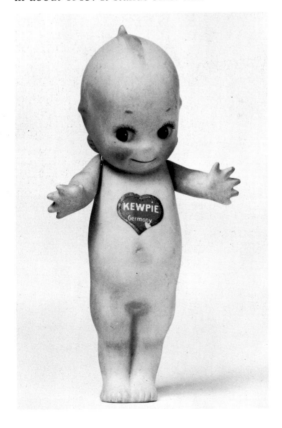

*Plate 4*

**Colour Plate 1.** *Glazed china shoulder heads, with painted facial features and moulded hairstyles. German, 1845-55, height 4ins. to 5¼ins.*

*Plate 5*

Plate 5 illustrates a celluloid doll, jointed only at the shoulders, with painted features. It was made by the Rheinische Gummi und Celluloid Fabrik of Mannheim and bears the company's trademark of a turtle (see Plate 30, p. 51). Made about 1900, the doll stands 18ins. high.

## Head and Torso Dolls

During the 18th century, wooden dolls were made from one block with separate arms and legs. The block was turned on a lathe to give the basic shape of the head, neck and limbless body to the hip line. Initially, the bodies were well carved, showing details of breasts and bottoms, but gradually the shape became stylised to form a rounded chest and square hip with a flat back. In a few cases, the maker did not bother to remove all the bark off the wood at the back or left it rather rough.

The wooden doll on the right of the Frontispiece represents a lady, with well defined carving to show a non-stylised face, breasts and a very narrow waist which extends down to a wide hip line. In common with most dolls it conforms to the fashionable shape of the day and the body has been made in the shape achieved by stays and corsets on the human body. This doll was made in England, between 1700 and 1720 and stands 19ins. tall. Various aspects of this doll are discussed throughout the book. Plate 6 (overleaf) illustrates the back of the doll and shows the carving of the narrow waist and bottom.

The wooden doll on the left of the Frontispiece is known as Sophie. This doll was also made in England about fifty years after the one on the right. If you compare the two, she has a very stylised, rather flat, face with the breasts indicated by a semi-circular chest. Her waist is round, stopping abruptly with the hips coming straight out at each side. She is altogether cruder, from her carving to her paintwork. This doll stands 24¾ins. tall. Various aspects of this doll are discussed throughout the book, and she will be referred to as Sophie.

Plate 7 (overleaf) shows Sophie's flat back, square hip line and flat uncarved bottom. The bottom also shows an area of rough wood which the maker did not attempt to smooth down.

The carving of wooden dolls gradually deteriorated and by the end of the 19th century, so crude had the carving become, that nose triangles were inserted into the face rather than carving out a nose from the block. The deterioration was shown in other aspects of the dolls' manufacture and are discussed throughout the book.

The same principle of a head and torso combination was also applied to cast dolls of other materials, china, bisque, celluloid and vinyl. The treatment of the facial features, however, was governed by the material.

With glazed china and bisque dolls, the facial features were moulded and painted, the hair could be treated in a similar manner

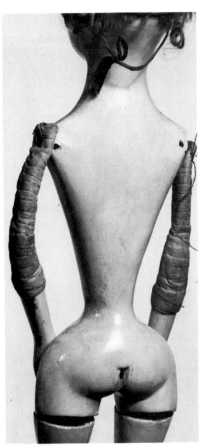

*Plate 6*

*Plate 7*

22

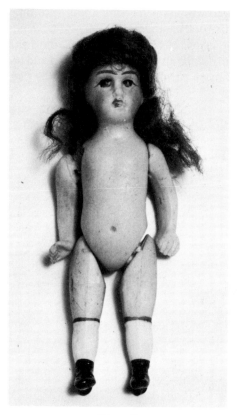

*Plate 8*

but often mohair was used. Likewise the eyes could be painted but glass eyes, whether stationary or sleeping, were used. Generally glazed china and bisque head and torso dolls were small and are often found in dolls' houses.

The bisque doll shown in Plate 8 has painted facial features and eyes, and mohair glued to the head. The lower legs have been painted to represent white and blue socks, while the feet have been moulded and painted to represent black, heeled shoes. At the top of each limb is a small loop moulded into the bisque through which is knotted the string for jointing. This doll was probably made in France between 1900 and 1910 and it stands 4ins. tall.

When celluloid was used to create a doll with a head and torso combination, the dolls are also generally quite small and in many cases their clothes are either sewn or glued onto them. Since the 1950s, many vinyl dolls are made with the head and torso combined and they are a more normal size for a doll to be played with by a child.

Plate 9 shows a vinyl doll, representing a baby with slightly bent limbs and painted features. This doll has its mouth in an open 'O' shape to take a feeding bottle; however, there is no outlet for the liquid in the body. This doll is marked 'Dollytex' and was made in Finland about 1960. She stands 13¼ ins. tall.

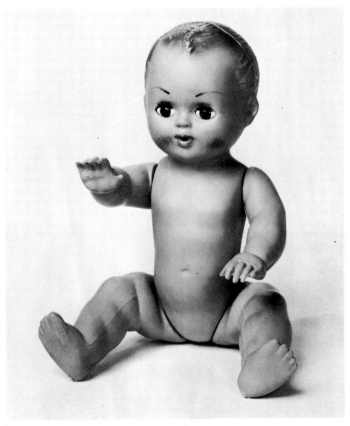

*Plate 9*

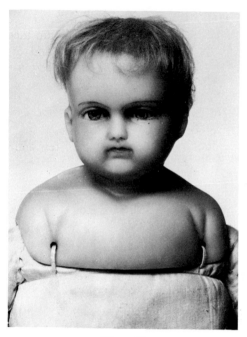

*Plate 10*

# The Shoulder Head

A shoulder head is created by casting the head with the neck, upper shoulders and front and back chest plates. They form a complete unit. The shoulder plate, the area from the base of the neck, extends to the sides only as far as the top of the arm, but in length it extends about one-third of the way down the upper chest. Throughout the 19th century and most of the 20th century, this shape of head was the most common form for wax, glazed china and composition, though wood, bisque and metal were also fashioned into the shape.

Plate 10 is of a wax doll, representing a baby, with glass eyes and hair inserted into the wax. The shoulder head shape was always used for poured wax heads as the material is fragile. This head style was strong with a sizeable area to cover the upper body which added support. It was attached to the body with thread sewn through the holes at the bottom corners of the front and back plates. On wax heads, these holes are generally lined with a metal eyelet to give additional strength. This doll was probably made by the Montanari family in England in about 1860. It stands 24ins. tall and the head is 6ins. Occasionally one will find a wax shoulder head which is glued on or held by a combination of sewing and gluing.

When wood is used to produce a shoulder head, it is carved from a single block, then painted, but the resulting shape looks the same. An example is shown in Plate 11. This wooden shoulder head, with painted facial features and hair, was made in Germany in about 1860 and is 3½ins. high.

*Plate 11*

Composition, when used as a wood substitute, was cast not carved. Likewise, when the composition was coated with wax, it was cast.

Plate 12 illustrates a composition shoulder head, with painted features and a human hair wig. It is mounted on a cloth body which stands 17½ins. tall. These heads were made in Germany between 1830 and 1837.

*Plate 12*

A wax over composition shoulder head is shown in Plate 13, with glass sleeping eyes and human hair inserted into the wax. It is mounted on a cloth body which stands 30ins. tall. The head was made in Germany about 1850.

Glazed china, bisque and metal shoulder heads are all cast, usually in two halves with the join running across the head, down just behind the ears, and over the crest of each shoulder.

As can be seen from Plate 14 (another view of the 'Dollytex' vinyl doll shown in Plate 9, p. 24) some cast seam lines were not properly cleaned. Although the head is neither a shoulder head nor one made from the materials already discussed, it has been used

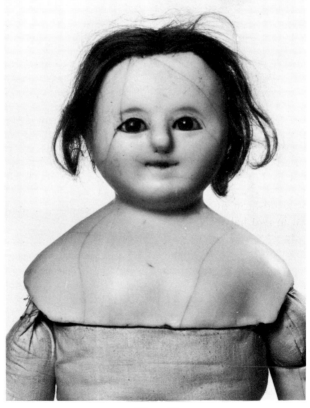

*Plate 13*

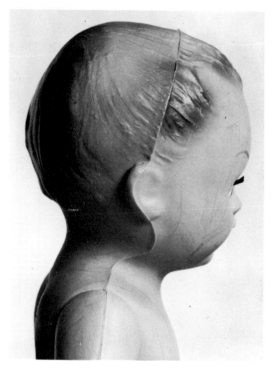

*Plate 14*

because the position of the cast lines, which applies to all dolls'
heads cast in two halves, is clearly visible.

Most shoulder heads have holes at the bottom edge of the front
and back plates. These holes are used when a head is sewn onto a
cloth body, though sometimes heads are glued to the body. At first,
the heads of glazed china had three holes in each plate but these
were reduced to two, one at each corner. These holes were marked
and needed to be punched out after the head had been fired.

Colour Plate 1, p. 19, shows glazed china heads, with painted
facial features and moulded and painted hair styles. The three
holed head is from about 1845 and 5¼ins. high; the middle sized
head is from about 1850 and 5ins. high; and the smallest head is
from about 1855 and 4ins. high. All four heads were made in
Germany. Notice the variation of colour from white to bright pink.

Plate 15 shows a bisque shoulder head, with glass sleeping eyes and a mohair wig. This head is glued to the kid body rather than being sewn. It was made by the German firm of Armand Marseille in about 1908. The total height is 29ins. and the head is 7ins.

The metal shoulder head in Plate 16 is made of tin painted with enamels, with glass sleeping eyes. This head bears the trademark 'Minerva' with a sign of a helmet on the front plate and the word

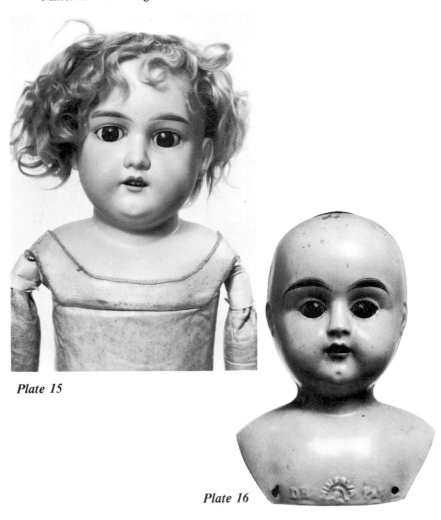

*Plate 15*

*Plate 16*

*Plate 17*

'Germany' on the back plate. It was made by the firm of Buschow and Beck of Reichenbach which also produced celluloid dolls. The trademark was registered in 1901 though in use from about 1894. The head is 4¾ins. high.

Occasionally makers decide to vary their designs and introduced more elaborate styles to their shoulder heads. The simplest was to indicate the breasts and their fullness. The more elaborate showed the frills of a chemise bodice and sometimes even neck ornaments. Most of these features may be seen in Plate 17 which shows a bisque shoulder head with painted features and moulded hair. The bases of both the front and back plates have been moulded and coloured white to look like the top of a chemise and around the doll's neck has been painted a decoration to represent a necklace which in fact matches the hair ribbon. The doll stands 16ins. tall and the head is 4ins.

# The Swivel Head

A variation of the Shoulder Head is commonly called the Swivel Head. Again there is a head and shoulder plate but the neck area is divided. The neck of the head ends in a ball shape which fits into a cup cast into the neck area of the plate. The two pieces are usually held together by a metal bar which runs from the head down into the body. The cup is usually lined with kid to prevent rubbing and scuff marks on the neck end of the head and to ensure a smooth movement.

This type of head was very popular with the French doll makers between 1860 to 1880 and many of the dolls of the period had these heads. Such a head allowed for finer modelling of the facial features and for individual positioning of the head.

Plate 18 illustrates a bisque swivel head, with glass eyes and a mohair wig. The head is mounted on a kid body and in fact it has been glued beneath the top edge of the kid. The front shoulder plate has been moulded to show the slight roundness of the bust

*Plate 18*

*Plate 19*

line and this roundness is just enough to create a swell in the kid. The doll stands 12ins. tall and the head is 3ins. This doll was made in France about 1870 to 1875. However, it was never played with and was found as part of the stock of a shop in Minster Gate, York.

One interesting point to remember while discussing swivel heads is that the very early English wooden heads of the 17th century also had divided necks though not with the elaborate cup and ball joint.

The wooden doll shown in Plate 19 was made about 1680. The head is attached with a length of metal running from the head through the body. This was revealed only within the last few years by X-rays. This particular doll is the one often called in books and articles 'the old Pretender'. The doll is known to have belonged to a member of the Scottish household of James, Duke of York, before he came to the throne as James II in 1685. The doll also went to St. Germain when he abdicated in 1688.

# The Socket Head

The Socket Head, like that of the swivel head, has a neck which ends in a ball shape. This fits into a specially designed cup shape, called a socket, at the top of the body. Socket heads were made from bisque and composition and the bodies designed for them were made of the same materials. However, it was not necessary for a bisque head to be matched to a bisque body, in fact most bisque heads were matched to composition bodies.

The socket head became the most popular style and both French and German makers used it. The majority of all bisque and composition dolls made from the late 19th century onwards are of this form. Celluloid was also used to make socket heads, and in some cases the same moulds were used for bisque and celluloid.

There were a number of advantages to this type of head. One of the main advantages was that it allowed for easier modelling so the variations in face style and expression grew. It became easier to produce the baby face, the child face or the adult face, faces that smiled and faces that were sad or thoughtful.

Plate 20 shows a bisque socket head, with glass eyes and a mohair wig. This head was made by the firm of Simon and Halbig of Grafenhein, one of the most prolific manufacturers working from the 1870s to the 1930s. The doll stands 14ins. tall and the head is 3ins. The body of this doll is discussed in the chapter on Bodies, and is shown in Plates 60 and 61 (p. 82).

# The Reverse Socket Head

During the 1920s and 1930s, some makers, particularly American ones, created a head with the ball and socket design reversed. The top of the body was extended to form the neck onto which sat the head which had the cup or socket.

A composition head with reverse socket head is illustrated in Plate 21. The doll has green metal sleeping eyes and a human hair wig. It bears the tradename EFFANBEE and was made by the firm of Fleischaker and Baum of New York in 1936. The doll stands 15ins. tall and the head is 3½ins. The doll is named Anne Shirley, after the heroine in *Anne of Green Gables*. The dolls were first introduced in 1935/36 and after 1950 were produced in plastic. The main features of these dolls are well defined large hands.

*Plate 20*

*Plate 21*

# The Flange Neck Head

Flange Neck Heads have necks which end with a slight ridge curving outwards. Usually teamed with a cloth body, the ridge fits under the neck edge of the body with the cloth drawn tight around it, thus making the head secure.

Plate 22 shows a glazed stoneware flange neck head, with painted features and moulded and painted hair. Below each ear and just above the ridge is a hole which can be used for additional stitching. This head represents a boy's head and it was made in England during the 1940s. It is 4ins. high.

More recently, vinyl dolls have had necks which end abruptly with or without ridges. Those head with ridges fit onto specially designed bodies with linking ridges.

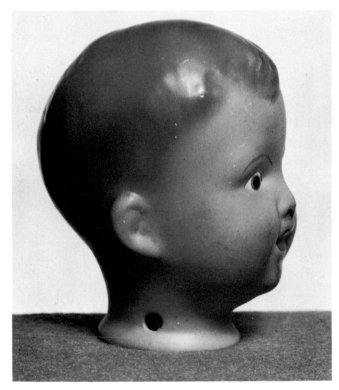

*Plate 22*

**Colour Plate 2.** *Bisque shoulder head, representing a boy, with painted facial features and hair. German, c.1868, height of head 3½ins.*

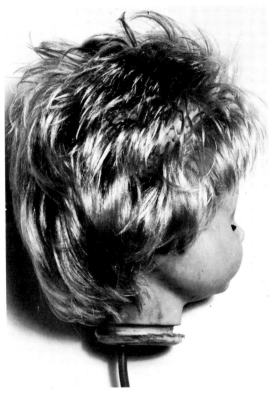

*Plate 23*

The soft vinyl flange neck head in Plate 23 has rooted nylon hair and plastic sleeping eyes. The ridge is well defined, though it had not been cleared of the extra waste vinyl produced during casting. This doll is a feeding doll and the pipe in the neck is attached to the mouth at one end and at the other end should be attached to a second pipe within the body. The doll was probably made in Hong Kong in the 1970s and the head is 5ins. high. This method of jointing is discussed on p. 134.

When you examine your doll, you are most likely to find that it has one of the head types discussed in this chapter. However, there are two major exceptions. The first exception is heads made of cloth which are discussed in Chapter 2, Materials. The second is a head with a face mask and this type is discussed in Chapter 5 on p. 169.

# *Chapter 2*
# Materials

Having decided which head type your doll has and even a possible date grouping, the next step is to decide what material was used to create the head. You will have noticed in the descriptions of the illustrations I have indicated the material used by a name — wood, glazed china, bisque, etc. Some of these names will be familiar while others are not. It is not at all easy to differentiate between the materials and the best guide is to study the head carefully and not to make a snap judgment.

## Wood

By its very presence and nature, wood has always been used to create dolls. It could be whittled, turned on a lathe, or carved to make either crude or elaborately styled faces and bodies, depending largely on the skill of the maker. For our purposes, we will be looking at wooden dolls made for commercial reasons rather than those dolls made at home for home use. A pinewood was the most common wood used as it was relatively easy to carve but not too soft.

It is probable that the 17th and 18th century wooden dolls described in this book were made in England. They have well documented backgrounds, though it is not possible to actually assign them to a known maker or even an area where they might have been made. The later wooden dolls described were almost certainly made in Europe as it is known that by the end of the 18th century, there was widespread importation of such dolls.

From the 17th century, four centres in Germany and Austria were making wooden dolls. These areas were the Grodener Tal region of Austria, now part of Italy, Sonneberg in Thuringia, and Oberammergau and Berchtesgaden, both in Bavaria. These were also the areas of the traditional toy making industry.

Throughout the period we are covering, you will notice that the carving and treatment of the wood changed and deteriorated.

Between 1680 and 1720, the dolls were of high quality, carefully carved with delicate paintwork. The whole of the body, as well as the head, tended to be given the same treatment. If you examine the doll on the right of the Frontispiece and in Plate 6 (p. 22), you will see paintwork which was created by preparing the wood with gesso, a thin layer of plaster. When the gesso was dry, the surface was painted and then given a top coat of varnish. In some cases, over the years the varnish has yellowed and the dolls now appear to be slightly anaemic. This is certainly not a problem to be worried about, just a question of age.

If you compare this doll with Sophie (left, Frontispiece and Plate 7, p. 22), you will immediately discover the differences between them . Sophie has a very flat stylised face with a crude body. Only the head, neck and upper chest has paintwork as described above. These are the areas which are visible when the doll is dressed. The rest of the body and the legs are painted matt white without the gesso base.

You will also see that the intricate carving of the earlier doll has been superseded not only by crudeness but also a stylised shape. Gone is the bust and the bottom, replaced by a semicircular chest and square hips.

By the 19th century when most of the manufacturing of wooden dolls was done in Germany and Austria, only the visible areas of the bodies were painted at all. Many of these dolls did not have the gesso base, the colours being applied straight onto the wood. The quality of paintwork matched the quality of carving and these were cheap dolls, not really designed or intended for preservation. Except for the earlier dolls, wooden dolls were given to young children to play with and many ended their days as the inhabitants of dolls' houses.

The two wooden dolls in Plate 24 are part of a group of seven made in the Grodener Tal, between 1925 and 1950. These dolls have paintwork only on the heads, necks, chests and lower arms and legs, while the rest of the body has been left bare. The group of seven range in size from 1in. to 11¾ins. It is this type of doll which is often called a 'Dutch' doll. The name maybe a corruption of the word Deutsch, meaning German, but as most of these dolls were imported via Holland, it is more probable that the name stems from this connection. It is also known that some of this type were assembled by Dutch wholesalers. The type is also known as a 'Peg-Wooden' and sometimes you come across a doll called 'The Smallest Doll in the World', which is a Dutch doll housed in a wooden egg. These dolls are very small, usually under one inch in height and they were bought as stocking fillers and cake decorations as well as toys.

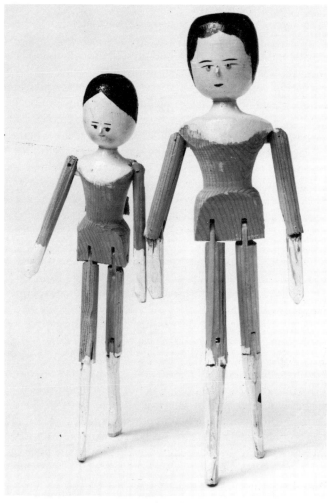

*Plate 24*

# Composition

Different mixtures, based upon wood or paper pulp, were developed as substitutes for wood. These new materials could be moulded and after moulding, their surfaces were excellent for painting. The collective name given to these materials is 'Composition', often because it can be extremely difficult to decide the exact mixture of the material.

The main composition used for heads and later for bodies was papier mâché. This was a mixture of very thin sheets of paper mixed with additives, then glued and pressed into moulds. The mixture was also treated with size, a glutinous wash giving a ground for the painting. Papier mâché is a strong material and is often found to have been used for making ornaments, boxes and even furniture.

At the beginning of the 19th century, makers found that the papier mâché could be moulded under pressure resulting in the first of the truly machine made, mass-produced heads. Makers developed their own recipes, usually kept secret, which included old rags, bread and crushed bones and eggs. These additives increased the strength and reduced the cost of the mixture. It is because these additives are known to have been used with the basic papier mâché that the term 'Composition' has been used and will be used in this book.

The first composition heads were generally shoulder heads, with a good finish. Later, socket heads were made, often from the same moulds as bisque heads. The heads could have moulded hair styles or wigs, and painted eyes or glass eyes. Basically, the finished head followed the style of those set by glazed china and bisque heads, which of course followed the fashions of the day.

If you look at Plate 12 (p. 27), this shoulder head, made from composition, has painted blue eyes and a human hair wig. There is no doubt that the head has been designed to represent a lady and it is delicate with high quality paintwork.

The main disadvantage of composition is that it is difficult to clean. The final paintwork was given a top coat of varnish which can be badly affected if touched by water. Soft, white bread gently rubbed over the surface will remove most of the dirt and dust without injury to the surface. However, should you attempt to try and clean it yourself, please remember not to scrub. This cleaning process will also work very well on composition bodies.

# Wax

There are three forms of wax heads — solid, poured and wax over composition. The basic material is bleached beeswax with additives such as red matter or pigment. It is probable that other substances were added and certainly makers now use a combination of various waxes, including paraffin. However, the recipes were jealously guarded secrets and for the purposes of the identification of a doll, it is not necessary to know the exact mixture. Wax is a beautiful but very difficult material to work with. It tended to give the most natural and human-like quality of all the materials used to make doll heads.

Solid wax heads can be created in two different ways, the first by simply carving a block of wax. The second way is to pour molten wax into a mould and leave it until the wax has set and hardened. The heads could have moulded hair styles or wigs, with painted facial features; however, the faces usually have fairly simple expressions and are rather round and flat. The eyes could be painted on but in most cases, the makers used small black beads stuck to the face.

Plate 25 (overleaf) shows a solid wax head, mounted on a cloth body. The head has been simply painted to show the facial features and the hair. No attempt has been made in moulding the hair, it is just created from a few lines of yellow paint. The eyes are black beads glued with a drop of molten wax to the head. The doll was probably made in England about 1810 and it stands 6ins. tall. The doll was contained in a blue cardboard box which was probably the original. Inside the box was an arc-shaped piece of padded yellow silk to be used as a head and neck cushion.

## Poured Wax

Poured wax heads are, as the name suggests, made also of molten wax poured into a mould. Before all the wax had set and hardened, the excess was drained off leaving only a shell. Some makers used several pourings to build up a thickish layer of wax. After the mould was removed the eye holes were cut out and the glass eyes warmed and attached by a small amount of molten wax to the inside of the head. After casting, eyebrows and lids were usually individually modelled, the painting completed and the hair inserted. It was the manufacturing of poured wax heads that was favoured

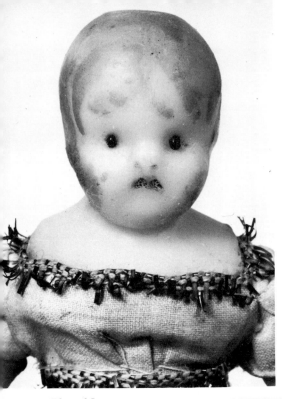

*Plate 25*

*Plate 26*

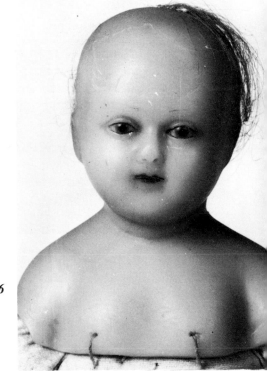

by English doll makers of the 19th century. They also used this method to create portrait dolls and the makers were referred to as wax modellers not doll makers.

The poured wax head in Plate 26, with glass eyes and mohair inserted into the wax, is mounted on a cloth body and the lower arms and legs are also of poured wax. The doll stands 13ins. tall and the head is 3ins. This doll was bought at the Dublin Exhibition of 1853 and it is marked 'Montanari Soho Bazaar'. The maker was Mme. Montanari, who with her son Richard, produced dolls in London from 1849 to 1884. Richard joined his mother in 1855 and continued making the dolls after her death in 1864.

## Wax Over Composition

Wax over Composition is the common term for the use of a wax skin over another substance which enhanced the look of the head while reducing its cost. The base material, usually composition, was moulded, then dipped into molten wax or painted with the molten wax. Sometimes the colour was on the base, to be covered with a white wax and sometimes the colour was applied to the wax. This can be determined by examining the edges of the shoulder plate where the wax is thinnest. Glass eyes were introduced in the same manner as wax heads, though glued with plaster rather than wax. As these heads were in fact stronger, they could withstand the use of sleeping eyes, either on a wire or with a lead weight.

The wax over composition shoulder head shown in Plate 13 (p. 28) has glass eyes which will open and close. In fact the eyes are operated by the pulling or pushing of a wire which protrudes from the body. Details of this eye movement are discussed in Chapter 5, p. 157.

With wax over composition heads and limbs, you might notice a crazing of lines or cracks. These are caused by the expansion and contraction of both materials occurring at different rates. Unsightly but quite normal, there is no need to worry unless a bit of wax comes away. However, should you notice any changes occurring to the wax, it is best to seek advice as soon as possible.

Wax is very susceptible to changes in heat, it will fade and even begin to melt if left in direct sunlight. It is also easily broken if knocked and dropped and care must be taken not to allow wax limbs to knock together. The noses of wax heads sometimes appear rather worn as if they have been kissed just once too often by their owners. This may well be the case but as noses protrude they do get rubbed even with the gentlest of treatment. It is never wise to attempt any cleaning or repairs to wax dolls. Such jobs, when absolutely necessary, should be carried out by an expert.

Wax heads have been popular throughout the 17th, 18th and 19th centuries and into the 20th century, though their styles and method of production have changed. There is now a revival of the art amongst present day makers, working with a beautiful, but rather difficult, almost temperamental substance.

## Glazed China

China is the common name for porcelain, a semi-translucent substance made primarily from kaolin, often called China Clay, a white clay produced by the decomposition of feldspar. This substance requires a very high firing temperature. On the whole, dolls made from glazed china are of German origin and are classified as being of hard paste porcelain. Dolls referred to as 'china' or 'glazed china' have a high glossy surface, not to be confused with those having a matt surface, termed 'bisque'. Throughout this book, I have called the china with the glossy surface 'glazed china'.

Though some glazed china dolls were produced during the 18th century, it was after 1830 when they reached their height of popularity. The dolls were often made by companies already producing china products; however, new doll manufacturers came into the market and many designers had their dolls made by long established firms.

Glazed china heads were cast in plaster moulds, which had been formed as negatives from a sculpted master. These moulds would be fit to do about fifty heads before they needed to be replaced. Early heads were formed by pressing the dough-like substance into the mould, firing it at a high temperature until it was set and then removing it from the mould. Later, a wetter mixture was poured into the mould with the excess drained off. The differences between the two processes can be seen on the insides of the heads, the first being uneven in thickness and much rougher. After the first firing, the heads were painted and glazed, then re-fired at a lower temperature.

Limbs were also made of glazed china to be used with cloth, wood and kid bodies. Whereas the heads might be tinted a flesh colour, limbs usually were left white except where the feet might be coloured to represent shoes.

The main characteristic of glazed china is that it is shiny and cool to the touch. The heads were made in the shoulder and swivel neck types. Because the heads were cast they lent themselves easily to having moulded hair styles, some styles being very elaborate with ringlets and combs. Earlier heads always have dark hair, brown or black, but gradually blond hair was introduced.

A glazed china shoulder head, with painted facial features and moulded and painted blond hair is illustrated in Plate 27 (overleaf). The head is mounted on a cloth body. The doll is one of those with an impressive head on an over stuffed body with short squat lower arms and legs mentioned in Chapter 1, p. 15. The doll was made in Germany and given as a present for Christmas 1888 or 1889 to a little girl called Gertrude Woods, born December 1882. See also the glazed china heads of Colour Plate 1 (p. 19).

## Bisque

Bisque is made from the same substance as the glazed china but is left unglazed, giving it a matt surface rather than a glossy one. After the initial firing, the painting of the surface and facial features was done, then the head was re-fired at a lower temperature to set the colours.

Most favoured by French and German makers, bisque remained the most popular substance for the creation of doll heads from the mid-19th century to the 1930s. The flexibility of design and treatment by the makers created dolls to represent ladies, children and babies. The heads were adapted from shoulder and swivel necks to socket and flange neck shapes, had painted eyes, glass eyes, and later sleeping eyes. So versatile were the designs that bisque has really only been replaced now by vinyl because of the cost and the new techniques of injection moulding.

Colour Plate 2 (p. 37) shows a bisque shoulder head, designed to represent a boy. The facial features and the hair are painted and the head is mounted on a cloth body. The doll was made in Germany about 1868 and it stands 15ins. tall and the head is 3½ins.

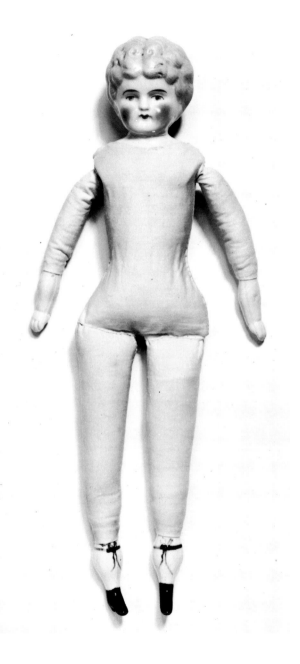

*Plate 27*

*Plate 28*

# Stoneware

Stoneware is a pottery made from a siliceous clay or one made with a mixture of clay with flint or sand. It is hard and dense but quite pale in colouring, and is non-porous when unglazed. Its surface is always rougher to look at than porcelain and it is not translucent. When ceramic dolls were made in England between 1914 and 1922, they were generally made of stoneware.

Plate 28 shows a stoneware shoulder head, designed to represent a girl. This is one of a set of three interchangeable heads which included a negro boy head and one set of pink limbs and one of brown limbs. The body on which any of the heads could be placed is of cloth with the stamp 'Exchange Dolls Protected'. The three heads are commonly termed 'character' heads and they have intaglio eyes and moulded hair. The head is 4ins. high. Each head is marked D.P. Co. with a set of numbers. The maker was a company called the Doll Pottery Company of Fenton, founded in 1916 and continuing until 1922. One interesting note is that the brown used to create the negro head is applied over pink stoneware.

The cloth body and stoneware limbs for the head in Plate 28 are shown in Plate 29. The body is stuffed as are the upper arms and thighs. The arms and legs are flanged and the loose cloth would be placed around the ridges and drawn tight. The head would be sewn on over the upper body. The body is 7½ins. long and each limb is 3¼ins.

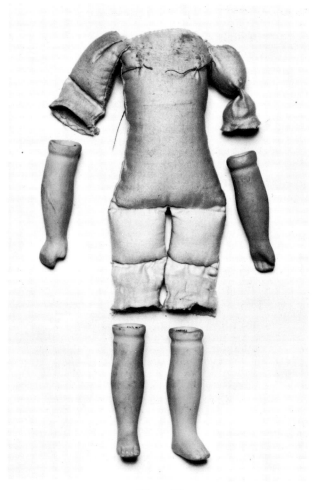

*Plate 29*

# Celluloid

A highly inflammable substance, celluloid, was developed by two brothers, James Wesley Hyatt and Isaiah Smith Hyatt, who owned a company called the Celluloid Novelty Company of Newark, New Jersey, USA. The tradename, Celluloid, was used from about 1869 and the material consisted of pyroxylin, a mixture of vegetable fibre impregnated with nitric and sulphuric acids, and added to camphor, pigments, fillers and alcohol. The trade name was later applied to all pyroxylin plastics regardless of manufacturer.

The majority of dolls made of this substance were produced by the Rheinische Gummi and Celluloid Fabrik, founded in 1873 in Bavaria. Doll makers would bring their designs to the factory to be moulded, and when this happened both the makers' marks and those of Rheinische would appear on the doll. The trademark of the company was a turtle, representing durability, and it was introduced in 1889 though not registered for ten years. This company is still active, now using only vinyls, and called Schildkrot Spielwaren GmbH. Schildkrot is the German word for turtle.

Plate 30 shows a pair of celluloid hands showing the turtle trademark, Germany as the country of origin, and the size number 4.

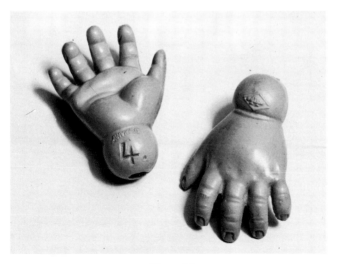

*Plate 30*

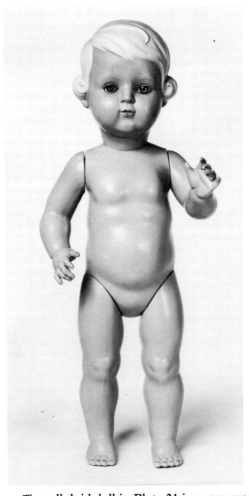

*Plate 31*

The celluloid doll in Plate 31 is a rare example of an all celluloid jointed doll with a socket head, glass sleeping eyes and moulded hair. Both the head and body bear the turtle trademark and the doll was probably made in the 1930s. She stands 19ins. tall.

Colour Plate 3 (p. 56) shows a celluloid head, which was probably cast in a mould designed for a bisque head. The doll has a kid body and it was made for the German firm, J.D. Kestner, about 1910. It stands 18ins. tall.

# Vinyl

A development from celluloid to produce a more flexible and non-inflammable material resulted in plastics made from hydrocarbon compounds collectively called vinyls. The first dolls which were made in the late 1930s were quite hard to the touch but the modern mass-produced ones have very soft, skin-like surfaces which are even warm to the touch.

However, vinyls have not proved as durable as they were first thought to be. Early examples have faded and discoloured and sometimes they have cracked. There is no solution to this at the moment but to try and keep the dolls away from heat and direct sunlight. Soft vinyls may not suffer in this way but as yet not enough time has elapsed to see the effect of aging.

The vinyl doll, with sleeping eyes and rooted saran (nylon) hair, shown in Plate 32, probably represents Miss Revlon. It was made by the Ideal Toy Corporation as an advertising project for Revlon Inc. of America. Made in 1956, it stands 10ins. tall.

*Plate 32*

A vinyl baby doll, completely made of soft vinyl, with sleeping eyes and rooted nylon hair, is shown in Plate 33. The doll was made in 1962 by H.G. Stone and Company of England. The doll, called a 'Chiltern Babykins', is 19ins. tall.

Both the dolls in Plates 32 and 33 have a number of garments which are very typical of the period and fashions of their day.

*Plate 33*

## Rag Dolls

Rag dolls come in many forms from home made to mass-produced ones. By their very nature, of all dolls these are the ones which have not survived in great numbers and they are also the ones which are most easily destroyed, thrown away or eaten by mice and insects.

A home made rag doll is often a baby's first doll, though it may not be in human form, but rather an animal or even an abstract shape. A mother could fashion a doll from some of her own garments or knit one from bits of old wool. The variety is endless, limited only by the imagination of the maker.

Commercially made rag dolls also vary enormously and only the main types which are likely to be found are discussed here. Should you have a rag doll which does not fit into these guidelines, please seek expert advice.

'Rag' is a general term to cover dolls of cloth and in turn 'cloth' is used to cover materials which are similar and not easily differentiated. In this context, 'cloth' will be used to cover linen, calico, cotton and muslin, but not felt, velvet or stockinet. Linen is woven from yarn made of flax, while cotton is of yarn from the cotton plant. Calico and muslin are both of cotton, the first being rather coarse and the second very fine.

Mass-produced cloth dolls have either painted or printed facial features. The printed ones came in sheets which had all the pieces to be cut out, sewn together and stuffed. Some were quite simple with only a front and back, while others were more intricate with separate parts of the body. These dolls, made throughout the 19th century (and still produced today) had flat faces and only slightly shaped bodies. They were stuffed with a variety of materials including other cloth, sawdust, kapok and latterly foam chips and old nylon stockings. Many rag doll sheets are being printed today and some are reprints from early designs. They are not fakes but reproductions and should have information about the original sheet as well as the *new date* of production. Take care that you are not misled into thinking you have an old doll when you acquire one of these sheets or the doll made from it. An example of a rag doll sheet is shown in Plate 34 (p. 57) in red, blue, yellow, pink and black. It was made in England between 1916 and 1920. While cloth is soft and warm, it has the great disadvantage of being difficult to clean and, if already dirty, of getting it clean. Also cloth can tear.

Not all rag dolls are of the sheet format; some doll makers used cloth to emulate jointed dolls. The greatest exponent of this was Kathe Kruse, who in 1910 created a doll which had more realism than the normal dolls of the period. Her production doll heads were made of three pieces of muslin with the inner surface chemically treated and stiffened and the outer surface painted with oils, then covered to make the surface washable. The heads and parts of the bodies were weighted with sand to give a more realistic feel to the dolls.

**Colour Plate 3.**
*Celluloid shoulder head, with a kid body, glass sleeping eyes and a mohair wig. Made by J.D. Kestner, German, c.1910, height 18ins.*

*Plate 34*

The Kathe Kruse Baby, designed to be a new born baby in a sleeping position, is shown in Plate 35 (overleaf). The muslin head is made and treated as described above and the body and limbs are of stockinet. One interesting attempt to increase the realistic look of the doll is the tummy button which the maker stitched from a tiny ring of stockinet (Plate 36). The doll has the maker's name stamped on its left foot sole and it stands 20ins. tall.

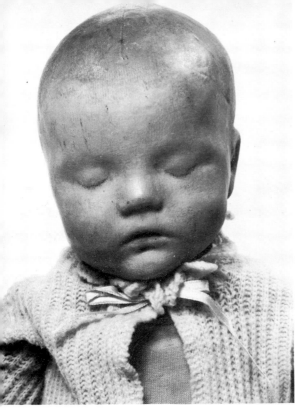

*Plate 35*

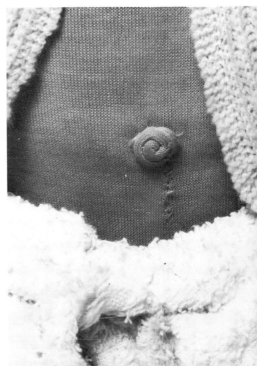

*Plate 36*

# Felt

Felt, another popular material, is a compact fabric made of wool fibres matted together under pressure. When treated for stiffening, felt becomes ideal to mould and facial features are raised rather than flat. The material was used by a number of makers including Elena Scavini, the creator of the Lenci Doll, Norah Wellings, and the English company, Chad Valley of Birmingham.

While facial features are generally found to be painted on felt dolls, glass eyes could be used and often the hair, be it silk, wool or mohair, was added on, either by sewing it directly to the head or by using a wig.

The Lenci Boy doll, shown in Plate 37, was one of a pair which was still contained in its original box. It was made in 1927 and the head is 4ins. high. This doll is discussed throughout the book and is shown in Colour Plate 10 (p. 181).

*Plate 37*

# Stockinet

Stockinet is a knitted fabric, made of silk or fine cotton. It has considerable elasticity and is generally to be found as a material for bodies.

The stockinet head shown in Plate 38, with the material stretched over a hollow papier mâché base, has been moulded to shape the facial features. These features have been painted and the hair style is created by yellow silk threads sewn to the head. The doll was made in France about 1920 and it stands 20½ins. tall.

*Plate 38*

# Velvet

Velvet, like stockinet, was a rare material in doll making but a few makers, notable amongst them Norah Wellings, did use velvet successfully to create heads and bodies.

Plate 39 shows a sailor, with a moulded velvet face and a velvet body. The facial features have been painted and the head is separate to the body and can be turned. The doll stands 16ins. tall. This doll wears a cap labelled 'S.S. OCEAN'. Norah Wellings produced these sailor dolls to be sold as souvenirs aboard ocean liners. The cap would have the name of the ship.

*Plate 39*

# Paper

The use of paper, other than that in papier mâché, is confined to Cut-Out Dolls, both home made and manufactured ones. Pre-1800, cut-out dolls were hand made and painted, but as printing processes improved, mass-produced sets began to appear. Produced on varying weights and qualities of paper, which were reflected in their cost, the sets reproduced current fashions.

Plate 40 shows a hand made cut-out set of 1788, consisting of a doll, nine dresses and three hats. All the pieces were hand coloured and were contained in a folder inscribed "Miss E. Hardy, Dresses for September 1788". The doll is 5ins.

*Plate 40*

*Plate 41*

In about 1810, one London publisher, S. and J. Fuller of London, produced sets of cut-outs to accompany small booklets of stories and poems. They had some quite intriguing titles such as "Ellen or the Naughty Girl Reclaimed" and "Phoebe, the Cottage Maid".

Plate 41 shows "The History of Little Fanny", also published by S. and J. Fuller in 1810. The set consists of seven cut-out figures of a girl in a variety of costumes to illustrate the scenes described in the booklet. The figures are all about 5ins. tall. You will notice with this set that only the head is separate. Usually called tab heads, the head extends down the neck in a triangular shape ending in a point.

Other publishers, including ones in France and Germany, also printed sets in connection with booklets. Not all the sets were about girls; many were done about boys with titles such as "Ernest ou Le Petit Robinson" by Augustin Legrand, 1821, and "The Genteel Boy and His Doings" by an unknown German maker about 1850. The latter set was double sided, that is to say that the figure and the

*Plate 42*

costumes showed the back as well as the front of the figures. "The Genteel Boy and His Doings" consists of a set of nine figures in a variety of costumes together with four hats, all contained in the original box. Some of these are shown in Plate 42.

Many companies used cut-out dolls as advertisements for their products and many magazines included sets to be cut from their pages.

Plate 43 shows "Jackie, Molly, Dolly and Joan", four of a set with their bases marked "Copyright 1923" and much of their clothing marked "Horrockses", to advertise the different materials made by the company. The dolls stand between 4¾ins. and 7⅜ins. tall.

Cut-out dolls still remain very popular, though now many are published in special books rather than in magazines.

Plate 44 illustrates a wedding group, complete with bride and groom and their attendants, flowers and a trousseau. The bride stands 9¾ins. tall.

Plate 43 ▲

▼ Plate 44

# Metal

Patents for metal heads were applied for in the 1860s, to create the heads from copper, zinc, brass, pewter, tin, lead and aluminium. The heads were generally cast in two halves, like a bisque head, then welded together before enamel paint was applied. The treatment for the eyes and hair followed the same guidelines as other materials.

Metal heads are often less attractive and, although the paint may chip if not handled with care, they are, of course, unbreakable. You will notice if you examine Plate 16 (p. 30) the Minerva metal head that the head has an open pate and the joins have not been completely sealed.

As well as Bushow and Beck who made the Minerva heads, many European and American manufacturers produced metal heads. Many also made doll parts and whole dolls of metal. These dolls, though not as popular as most of the other types, continued to be made until the 1930s.

# Colour

We have been discussing the materials used to make various dolls but within each type of material you will notice that the colour varies considerably, from white to purplish pink. This, of course, excludes those dolls which were intended to represent a Negro or Oriental doll. Initially the colour was determined by the maker. In the case of dolls made of glazed china or bisque, the colour varies from white with bright red, blue and black facial features, to the rosy pink with more tempered colours for the features. Because of the type of material and the firing of the colours, the colours of the doll will not have changed.

Wax, on the other hand, is affected by external factors; light, heat and sometimes even the dyes used in the clothes. Probably the most common result is the whitish face with pink retained on the neck and chest, but occasionally, the chemicals used to produce the original colour are affected and these darken rather than lighten to a purplish hue.

With a material which has been painted and then varnished, the result can be a jaundiced appearance caused by the yellowing of the varnish. Fabrics are most affected by dirt and insects. There is really no way to change, clean or repair most of the damage which has already occurred to the colour, but as the guardian of your doll, it is up to you to ensure that the process of deterioration is stemmed as much as possible. Try to house your doll in a clean, dust proof case, surrounded by acid free tissue or card, and away from direct sunlight, hot water pipes and radiators. A few precautions will allow you to enjoy your doll without the constant worry or her welfare.

One interesting note is that you might dig up a bisque or other ceramic head in a garden. Ceramics buried in the ground often lose their colouring, even though that colouring has been fired onto the surface. This is caused by a chemical reaction with the components of the soil which can also cause mottled stains on the surface of the head.

# *Chapter 3*
# The Bodies

## Body Shape

Strange as it may seem, the adult female body has been the commonest body shape used throughout the three hundred years we are covering. The shape is really only a suggestion showing the roundness of the breasts, waist, hips and bottom, though very occasionally you will see a doll with these features positively indicated. It is also rare to find a male body portrayed on European dolls, though the male body is commonly found on dolls from Central and South America, Japan, South East Asia and the Middle East.

The adult body, though only a suggestion, did change its shape over the years. The changes, attempted by the use of corsetry on the human figure, were achieved by cutting, shaping and padding on the doll. It is not possible to mould the shape on a doll as it is with humans, so the desired shape had to be created. Also, while foundation garments were used when dressing a doll, it was practical to provide a little assistance so on some dolls, for instance 'fashion' ones, an exaggerated bottom and very narrow waist can be found showing the ideal shape required by the dictates of the fashion of the day.

If you look at the doll on the right of the Frontispiece, you will see that this doll makes no bones about the fact that she represents an adult woman. However, if you study Plate 6 (p. 22) showing the doll's back, you will notice that it is formed into the 'idealised' fashion shape of the day with a very narrow waist and almost forming a 'V' at the front.

If you compare Sophie to her earlier friend, Frontispiece (left) and Plate 7 (p. 22), you will see that her body is much more stylised — gone is the bosom, the waist and the bottom. Sophie is the shape of most dolls of the 18th century and if you also compare her with Plate 24 (p. 41), you will see much of the deterioration of design and form which had occurred by the 20th century.

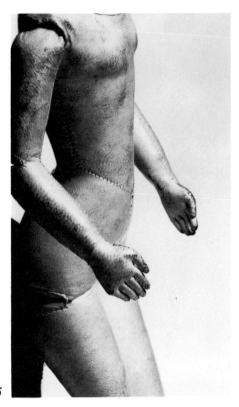

*Plate 45*

Plate 45 shows a kid body, designed, cut out, stitched and padded to provide the ideal shape of the 1870s and of the fashionable doll. The doll also has gussetting at its joints for partial movement. This is the body of the head shown in Plate 18 (p. 32) where you can see the slight indication of the breast. Colour Plate 4 (p. 73) shows a dressed version of the gussetted kid body which was designed to give the ideal fashionable shape of the 1870s. This French doll has a bisque swivel head with glass eyes and a human hair wig. She stands 12ins. tall.

The composition body in Plate 46 was designed for a Simon and Halbig adult head of about 1900. The body shape is quite stylised but on the whole more feminine than many of the earlier ones of both the 18th century and the 1870s. The doll is also quite slight in

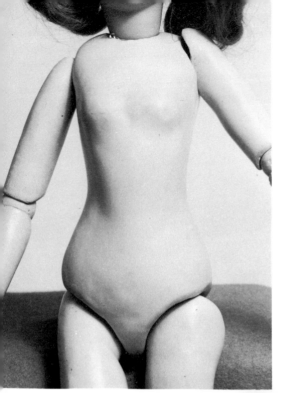

*Plate 46*

*Plate 47*

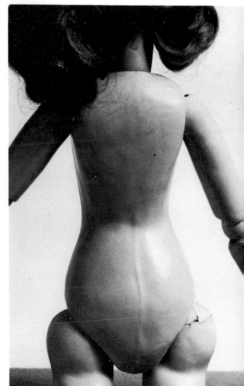

appearance and stands 15ins. tall. The back view is illustrated in Plate 47 showing the overall shape and the moulding seam.

The 'baby' body was developed during the 19th century, first using stuffed cloth and later composition and other materials. These bodies tended to be chubby and round with 'pot belly' stomachs. Sometimes they were without any shaping, almost square in appearance, but other bodies, particularly when made of composition, had been designed to create the actual human shape.

The stuffed cloth body in Plate 48 was designed for a poured wax head which was probably made by Richard Montanari about 1865. The body has no shaping of any kind and would be only suitable for being dressed as a baby. The doll also has poured wax lower arms and legs, blond mohair inserted into the head and glass eyes. It stands 24ins. tall. This is the doll shown in Plate 10 (p. 25).

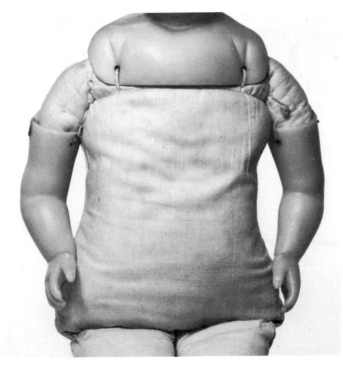

*Plate 48*

The stuffed cloth body in Plate 49 was designed for a poured wax head made by Thomas Peacock of London. The mark is stamped on the chest. Although this body is shaped to show a waistline, the doll was dressed as a baby and the face is rather baby like. It is probable that bodies of this type were used with both adult and baby heads as under long robes the shape could not be distinguished. It is also probable that the doll could be dressed as a baby, a child or an adult, as many of the faces made could be classified as all-purpose designs. The choice of clothing would then be up to the owner.

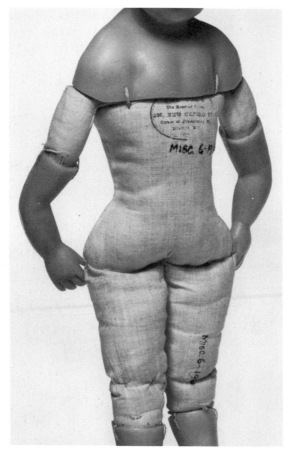

*Plate 49*

***Colour Plate 4.***
*Bisque swivel head,*
*with a kid body,*
*bisque hands, glass*
*eyes and a human*
*hair wig. French,*
*c.1870, height 12ins.*

Plate 50 shows a composition body, designed for the character head made by Gebruder Heubach of Germany about 1910. The body has a more realistic form than the two cloth ones in Plates 48 and 49 and the limbs used with it are bent to complete the illusion of a baby shape. This doll stands 15ins. tall and it is further discussed on p. 152.

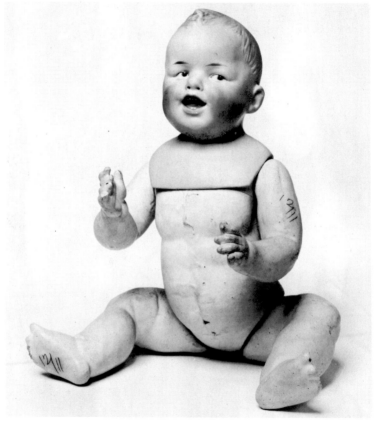

*Plate 50*

The 'child' body was designed to be thinner, a more elongated form than the baby body but without the finer shaping of the adult one. These bodies are often called 'toddler' and in many cases the limbs used with them are absolutely straight.

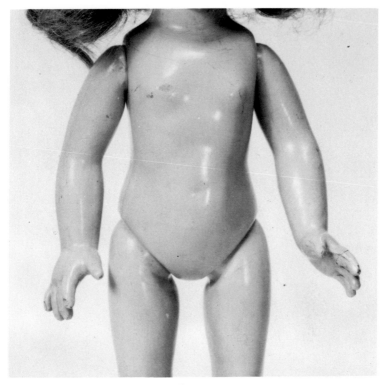

*Plate 51*

Plate 51 shows a composition toddler body, designed for the Anne Shirley doll in Plate 21 (p. 35). This particular body, first introduced in 1935, was later used with other heads. One of the main features are the large, well shaped hands. The doll stands 15ins. tall.

You will find, should you try to dress a doll in real children's clothing, that dolls were decidedly healthier than their human counterparts. You will probably experience difficulty in even getting the clothes on or done up.

The distinction between an adult and a teenager seems to be a recent social development, an invention of the post war years, and

*Plate 52*

dolls were created which reflect this change. The Barbie doll, introduced in the USA in the late 1950s, probably had the major impact in creating the teenage doll and many dolls of this type followed, each with a popular, easy to remember name and endless accessories — houses, cars, animals, swimming pools, as well as innumerable changes of clothes.

Plate 52 shows a Sindy doll, in this case the New Active Sindy ballerina, designed by Pedigree of England. The doll is made entirely of vinyl with painted facial features, rooted nylon hair and moveable joints. The doll stands 16ins. tall.

# Design of the Body

When a doll's body was designed, many additional features other than the shape had to be considered. Provision had to be made for the type of head used, the jointing required and the mobility desired. Of course, for the head and torso combination, there was no need to design a special neck. Likewise for the shoulder and swivel heads, no special treatment was required except provision of a solid foundation to which the head could be stuck or sewn. However, for the other types of heads, the bodies had to be adapted.

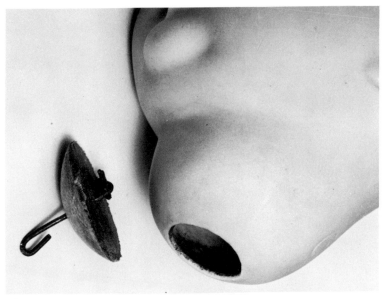

*Plate 53*

Socket heads, almost exclusively using composition bodies, fitted into cups or sockets at the top of the torso. These cups were strengthened with wood or thick composition as the pressure and the tension from the jointing was considerable. Plate 53 illustrates the neck socket hole of the doll shown in Plate 20 (p. 35) with a metal and wood hook for stringing. The body is composition and designed to take a bisque socket head.

Frequently seen on more recent dolls is the Reverse Socket Neck. The roles of the head and the body neck areas have been reversed so the head has the cup or socket and the neck of the body extends to form the ball. An example is shown in Plate 54 with a composition head. The composition body is a toddler type and the doll was designed to represent the child star, Shirley Temple. It was made by the Ideal Novelty and Toy Company and was introduced in 1934. She stands 22ins. tall and a full view of the doll is shown in Plate 69 (p. 95). This doll continued to be made after 1945 using vinyl rather than composition.

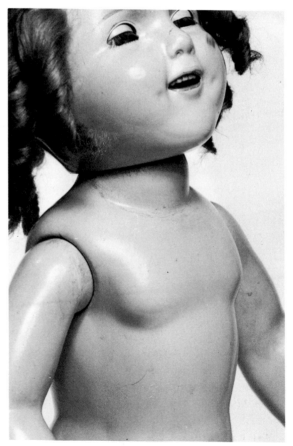

*Plate 54*

*Plate 55*

Flange heads were generally mounted on cloth bodies with the neck ridge of the head covered with the neck opening of the body which was stitched and drawn tight. Plate 55 shows a flange head on a cloth body. The base of the neck has a ridge over which the cloth of the body is shown.

Later flange heads, when made of vinyl, had a moulded groove which slotted into a matching groove on the body, as did the legs. (See Plates 23, 110 and 111, pp. 38 and 135).

It has always been desirable for dolls to have some movement and there were attempts to create more natural movements which affected the lower torso and the limbs. The torso had to be shaped so that the legs could bend at right angles to the body. Over the three hundred years, makers tried many different ways to produce the desired effect. Some worked very well and were quite good to look at, while others did not work and looked very odd. Of course, it was not always the good looking joints that worked the best.

On 17th and 18th century dolls, this desired leg movement was accomplished by suspending the legs below the torso. This leg

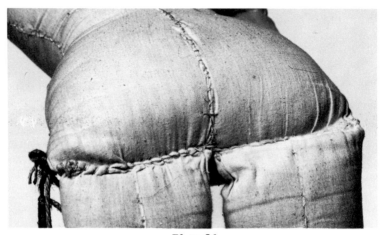

*Plate 56*

arrangement can be seen on most wooden dolls regardless of when they were made. The hinge of the leg joints are more fully described in the chapter about limbs.

The idea of suspending the legs was also used for cloth dolls, where the top of the leg was sewn to the base of the torso.

Plate 56 shows a cloth body with the legs suspended and stitched to the base of the torso. This is the body of the doll in Plate 13 (p. 28), whose wax over composition head was made in Germany about 1850.

The first major change to the use of suspended legs was the gusset. Seen on most kid bodies, a large gusset was placed at the base of the torso and attached to the top of each leg. When the doll was standing, the gusset folded inside the area between the bottom and thigh. When the doll was sitting, the gusset stretched out so that the legs could point straight ahead. A gusset could also be used at the knees so that the legs would bend.

Plates 57-59 show the gusset in the closed position for a doll standing up, the gusset in the open position for a doll sitting down, and the front of the lower torso showing the creased but unbroken line of the joint. As you will notice the gusset is formed like a patch, almost circular and stitched with very small but strong stitches around the outer edge. These three illustrations are of the body of the doll shown in Plate 18 (p. 32).

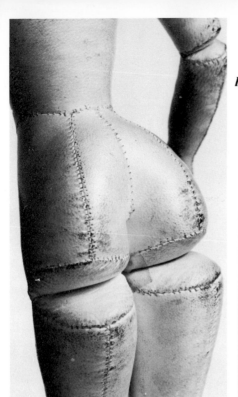

*Plate 57*

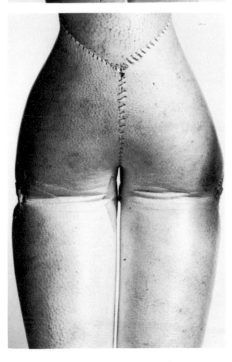

*Plate 59*

*Plate 58*

81

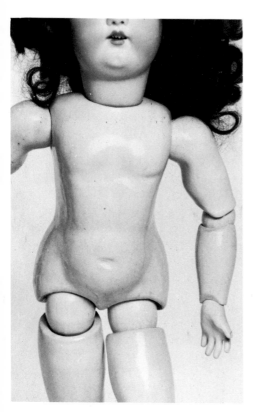

*Plate 60*

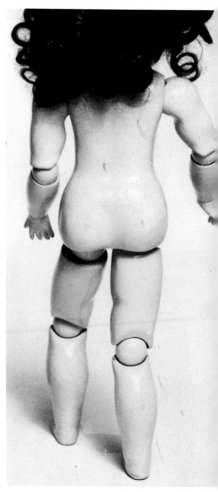

*Plate 61*

When a composition body was designed for a socket head, the rest of the body was generally designed to have ball and socket jointing for the limbs. Therefore the side of the shoulders and the base of the torso had sockets or cups like that provided at the neck. Sometimes the cups were right at the bottom of the torso but in most cases, the back extended further than the front and the cups appear at a slight angle. Occasionally the cups are at such an angle that they appear to be actually going up the front of the torso.

Plate 60 shows the front of the body of the doll in Plate 20 (p. 35). You will see that the cups for the legs are placed quite high in the base and if you compare this with Plate 61 you will see that from the back the doll shows no indication of the cups.

The treatment of arms was much simpler than that of the legs and required almost no design changes on the body except in the cases of the jointed wooden dolls and the composition dolls with ball and socket joints. Arms are discussed in connection with their shape and the jointing in Chapter 4, on pages 98-112.

## Materials

Although the materials used to make bodies are the same as those used for the heads, in many cases the head and body of one doll may be of different materials. Normally wooden heads have wooden bodies; wax heads have cloth ones; composition, glazed china and early bisque heads have kid or cloth bodies; later bisque heads have composition bodies; and heads of celluloid and other plastics have bodies of the same materials. These are only guidelines as almost any combination of head, body and limbs can be found.

Please read Chapter 2 for additional information about the properties of different materials.

## Wood

Wood has been used for bodies throughout the period covered but latterly not for large dolls, being replaced by lighter, more malleable materials. Generally these bodies have minimal paintwork, a coating of white or pink, as the body remained hidden under clothes. If you compare the dolls in the Frontispiece, the paintwork of the earlier doll (right) covers the whole of her body and legs while Sophie (left) has only a complete coating on her head and upper chest. Only if it was necessary was the upper chest painted and varnished properly to match the head so dresses with low necklines, for example, could be worn. If you also compare Sophie to the dolls in Plate 24 (p. 41), she was partly painted over the rest of her body, just a basic white matt coat, whereas the later dolls have no paint on the majority of their bodies or their upper limbs. They are only painted on areas which could show when the doll was dressed.

Glazed china and bisque shoulder heads are often found on wooden bodies but they are generally under 8ins. tall. Many are

*Plate 62*

now found as inhabitants of dolls' houses. Wax heads are not suitable for use on wooden bodies; wax was simply too fragile.

Unless they were moulded with the head to form an All-in-One doll or a Head and Torso doll, it is quite rare to find a large wax, glazed china or bisque body, and wax was never used to make a separate body.

The baby doll in Plate 62 is a good example of a doll with its head, body and limbs made of bisque. The firm of J.D. Kestner of Waltershausen advertised a doll called "Natural Baby" and this example, complete with a fine label on its chest, is one of this type. It is 6ins. tall and was made between 1912 when Natural Babies were first advertised and 1914 when this doll was bought.

## Cloth

The second mainstay for making doll bodies was cloth; though in many different styles and fabrics. The earliest we are considering are to be found in a German dolls' house dated 1673. There are ten

*Plate 63*

dolls in all, each with a body of narrow linen strips bound around a metal or wood frame. Their faces are wax masks stitched to the head area. The dolls range in size from a 2ins. baby to an 8ins. adult, but all their faces are about the same diameter.

Plate 63 (p. 85) shows the underneath of one of the dolls' house dolls showing the bound legs.

As their development became more sophisticated, cloth bodies began to resemble the human form. Made from calico or linen, and either pale pink or white in colour, the bodies were prepared from shaped pieces sewn together and stuffed with horse or cow hair, sawdust or kapok. Kapok is a fine cotton wool, also known as silk cotton, and it is more resilient to attacks from insects. However, it is expensive and unless packed very tightly, tends to lose its shape. Most cloth bodies had a front and back piece slightly shaped to narrow at the waist line. The two pieces were sewn together down each side and across the bottom with the top left open to allow for the stuffing to be put in. As most cloth bodies, certainly before this century, were intended for shoulder heads, the final sewing at the top was done in large stitches.

Cloth bodies were left untreated but very occasionally the upper chest and neck were above the dress edge and the area had to be painted and varnished to match the head.

The poured wax head with a cloth body in Colour Plate 5 (p. 92) has glass eyes and a human hair wig. Because the neck of the dress was low on the chest, the body area had been painted and varnished to match the wax head. Unfortunately with the passage of time, the wax has bleached while the cloth has yellowed. The doll bears a label which states she is dressed in a "Long robe coat for a lady of sixteen, 1758". This doll is one of a series dressed between 1757 and 1911 by members of the Powell Family, who dressed a doll each time an important event occurred in the family such as a wedding. This doll stands 13ins. tall.

With the introduction of the flange heads, the neck lines of cloth bodies had to change so they could be drawn tight around the base of the head. This can be seen on the cloth upper limbs of Plate 29 (p. 50).

Stockinet was also used for bodies and in the example in Plate 64 it was used to create a very shapely one indeed. This is a Gesland stockinet body with a bisque swivel head and lower arms and legs. Within the body there is a metal framework which allows some movement of the waist and the limbs. The framework has been padded with kapok, then covered with the stockinet. The doll's head bears the initials FG and was probably made by F. Gaultier of Paris about 1880. The body, known as a Gesland, is thought to be the type designed and made by the Parisian, Gesland. This doll is 18ins. tall.

The French boudoir or lady dolls of the 1920s were usually made from stockinet but these dolls were not generally of plain cotton stockinet, but of the silky variety made of mercerised cotton. This type of doll is shown in Plate 38 (p. 60)

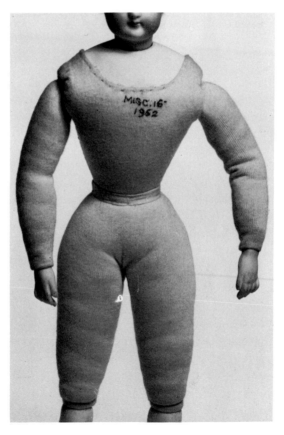

*Plate 64*

Felt was sometimes used for doll bodies. Originally the dolls made by the Lenci Company of Italy had moulded felt bodies; however, these were gradually replaced with cotton torsos and felt shoulders.

Plate 65 shows a Lenci felt body machine stitched down the back and across each shoulder and hand stitched between the legs. The body has been lightly modelled and it is not stuffed. This doll was made in 1927.

Plate 66 shows a Lenci felt and cloth body. By retaining the felt at the shoulders and for the legs and arms, the doll could be dressed in low neck line clothes and bare limbs and this principle follows that seen on the painted wooden dolls. This doll was made about 1935 and stands 18½ins. tall. The illustration shows the hip joint with the cloth body and felt legs.

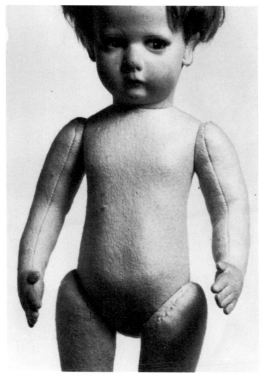

*Plate 65*

*Plate 66*

*Plate 67*

The use of cloth, be it cotton, linen, stockinet or felt, is still widely favoured by craftsmen making dolls today of traditional materials, but cloth bodies are not used with vinyl heads.

The cloth body in Plate 67 is for the doll called Willie, the All American Boy, designed and made by the Willie Wistful Doll Company in 1979. The doll stands 16ins. tall.

# Composition

Composition bodies were moulded from exactly the same combination of paper and wood pulp materials as the heads, though bodies were a later development and came to the forefront in the 1880s. From that time until 1940, composition bodies remained the most popular body type.

Composition bodies were hollow, cast in two halves, a front and back, then joined. As they were cast in a mould, as much or as little detail could be included and many of the pre-1914 bodies were very lifelike. In the twenty-five years that followed, the making of composition bodies deteriorated as did their appearance, shape, finish and paintwork.

The doll in Colour Plate 9 (p. 164) has a Jumeau bisque socket head with jointed composition body. This is a well modelled and painted body of the mid-1880s. There has been some discolouration of the body. Note the slight purplish hue, which is a common feature of dolls by this maker. The doll stands 20ins. tall.

The doll making factory of Jumeau was founded by Pierre François Jumeau in 1842 and continued until 1899 under his son, Emile. In 1899, Jumeau became a founding member of the Société Française de Fabrication de Bébés et Jouets. Until joining the society, the factory produced all the doll components, but during the early years of this century gradually began to use doll heads made in Germany.

The composition doll in Plate 68 was made about 1923. If you compare this body with that shown in Plates 60-61 (p. 82), you will see immediately the differences in both the quality of the modelling and the quality of the paintwork. These changes in the bodies reflected the cost, the ability of the maker and even the interest of the maker, and of course, the person who applied the paint.

The deterioration in the manufacture of composition bodies reached its lowest point by the 1920s and 1930s with the production of very cheap bodies made from a cardboard. Often called 'carton' bodies, the pieces were held with staples which have in many cases rusted and damaged the joins. These bodies are also very susceptible to being crushed.

It must be remembered that bodies were not made by the company or person who made the head, though many firms did work

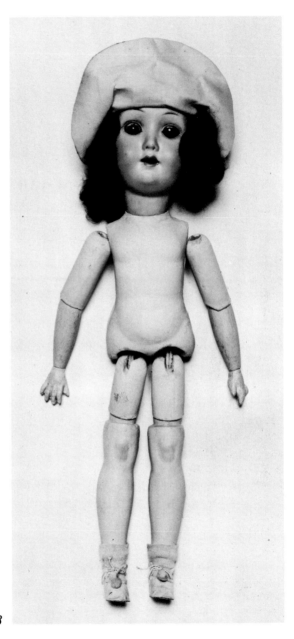

*Plate 68*

**Colour Plate 5.** *Poured wax head on a painted cloth body, glass eyes and a human hair wig. English, 1758, height 13ins. The doll is dressed in a "long robe coat for a girl of sixteen".*

together to produce a head and body that matched, such as Simon and Halbig, and Kammer and Reinhardt, who between them produced some of the finest bisque headed composition bodied dolls of the early part of this century.

Having cast the composition body, it was strengthened inside with wooden dowels acting as braces just below the shoulder and at the hip line. The surface of the body was painted with water based paints, sometimes over a gesso base though the composition formed a good painting surface. After the final colour coats, the whole surface was varnished. The colour of most composition bodies is a variety of pink unless the doll was intended to represent another race, in which case the body would be appropriately coloured.

## Damage

While talking of composition bodies, it is worth saying a few words about damage that may have occurred. Unless you are very unfortunate and the body has been dropped and stepped on, thus crushed, the damage to composition bodies occurs at the joins of the two halves and at the sockets, particularly where they are reinforced with wood. Damage might consist only of marks where the head and limbs have been turned and the varnish coat has worn. Usually, however, there will be small areas where the composition is cracked or even broken away. The worst damage is where the reinforcements have caved in, allowing the limb affected to slip into the body. The pressure used with the jointing is very great and care must be taken when tightening loose elastic or when restringing.

Damage to other types of bodies varies, depending on the material. Wood and cloth or kid bodies stuffed with sawdust are susceptible to woodworm, while moths like hair and wool padding. Of course, time itself ages and rots fabrics. Nevertheless, it is surprising that a dressed doll which has rarely been played with can have a body almost as clean as the day it was made and a body which looks too dirty or very mottled is suspect. This always suggests that an artificial aging process has been used.

# Chapter 4
# The Limbs

As with the head and the body, the shape of the limbs is largely determined by the type of doll, the age of the person it represents, and the materials used for its construction. It would look very silly if an adult head was placed on a round baby body. Nor would it be sensible to construct a doll with limbs either too large or too small; however, most dolls do have proportionately larger heads to the limb size. In most cases, the head was considered the major component and was thus treated as such. It must also be remembered that the body and limbs did not always match the sophistication of the head, nor were they as well finished.

When considering the limbs, there are two general type of arms and legs. The first is the complete limb, in one from fingers to shoulder or from toes to hip. The second type is the divided limb which may be in three sections.

## The Complete Arm

The complete arm is rarely seen on early wooden dolls or late, large wooden ones unless very cheap and crudely made, but is to be found on some Steiner walking dolls which are jointed at the shoulder with a bar. It is, of course, used on the rigid All-in-One dolls and sometimes on jointed glazed china or bisque dolls but only when they are small dolls or designed to represent babies. See Plates 2 and 62 (pages 17 and 84).

The Shirley Temple doll in Plate 69 has a toddler body and a complete arm. The doll is shown in Colour Plate 13 (p. 212).

When kid is used the arm may be complete but it normally has an elbow gusset and should be really classified as a divided arm. (See Plates 75 and 76, p. 101.)

It is in the arm made of composition and latterly vinyl where we see the greatest use of the complete arm section. Such arms would normally be seen on a baby doll or on one representing a young

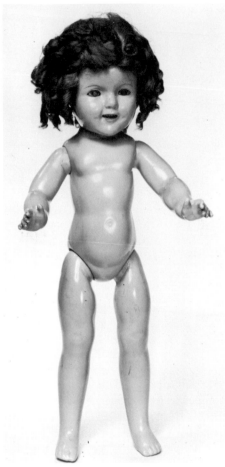

*Plate 69*

child. The 'baby arm' is slightly curved forward and that for a young child is straight. The shapes, which should match those of the legs, give rise to the general terms Bent Limb and Toddler. These terms describe the desired shape and give a vivid picture of the doll.

The doll in Plate 70 (overleaf) shows a bent limb complete arm section, made of composition. This doll was made after 1913 by the German firm of Franz Schmidt. The doll stands 22ins. tall. This doll is discussed further in Chapter 7, page 187.

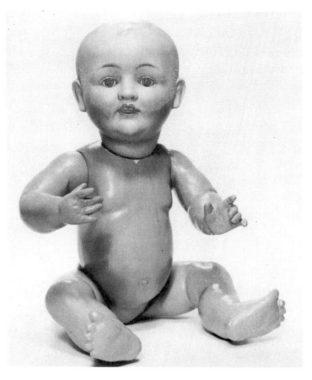

*Plate 70*

If you look again at Plate 51 (p. 75), you will see the use of the composition complete arm in the toddler shape. In the case of both the bent limb and the toddler arm, the elbows are normally indicated by a slight lump with a dimple at each side.

Plate 71 shows a bent limb complete arm made of soft vinyl. Another view of this doll, the Chiltern Babykins, is shown in Plate 33 (p. 54).

The shoulder end of the complete arm should be shaped to fit into the shoulder of the body which may be a socket or a flange. It must be shaped for easy jointing and to give a smooth line when in position. Composition complete arms have a metal hook embedded into the shoulder for the elastic stringing and vinyl ones will have either a self-hook or a ridge which fits a matching ridge in the body as a flange joint. This method of jointing is shown later in this chapter when dealing with the legs.

Complete arms of composition and vinyl are cast in moulds in the same manner as heads and bodies, but they are usually cast as one unit, not in two halves requiring joining. In some cases, and this also applies to bisque and china arms, while the finishing of the arms is good, you can see the mould line which runs along the back of the arm in line with the small finger and along the front of the arm in line with the thumb.

The production of complete arms from glazed china, bisque and wax followed the dictates of the body and it is rare to find examples. However, if you look at Plate 62 (p. 84), you will notice that the Kestner baby has bisque bent limb arms and legs, but it is a very small doll.

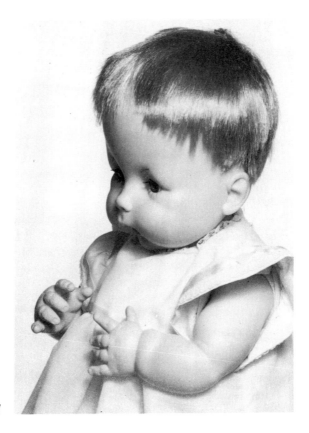

*Plate 71*

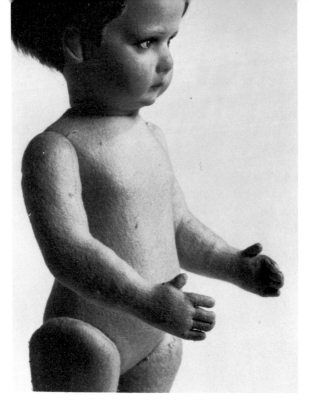

*Plate 72*

The majority of dolls made completely from a cloth of one kind or another have complete arms. Sometimes the arms are part of the body but they can be separate as seen on Lenci dolls.

Plate 72 shows a complete arm made of felt. In the case of this Lenci doll the shoulder area is supported inside and then attached to the shoulder allowing the arm to move. The hand is well formed with the fingers indicated by stitches. On other rag dolls, particularly those which are of printed cotton, the fingers may only be indicated by the printing or by the shape. Details of hands are discussed later in this chapter.

## The Divided Arm

When the arm is divided, the division is normally at the elbow, but sometimes a little higher or lower depending upon the look desired. Occasionally one will find an arm divided only at the wrist. Initially, we will concentrate on the upper arm and progress through the types and materials.

Wooden dolls of the 17th and 18th centuries had upper arms

made of strips of linen wound around to the desired length, as shown in Plate 6 (p. 22). The arm could also be of a linen stuffed with sawdust or hair. If you look at Plate 7 (p. 22) showing the back view of Sophie, you will see the linen upper arm; however, due to the ravages of time her arms are no longer stuffed. When a doll which had either of these upper arms was dressed, the linen area was covered by the dress material to form the sleeve.

The covered upper arm in Plate 73 shows the sleeve of the dress plus the muslin chemise sleeve. The doll was made about 1748.

On later wooden dolls, the upper arms were also made of wood, usually left unpainted, as shown in Plate 24 (p. 41).

*Plate 73*

*Plate 74*

Stuffed cloth upper arms were also used with cloth bodies regardless of the head material. They would be sewn to the body at the shoulder line.

Plate 74 shows a stuffed cloth upper arm, sewn to the body and caught beneath the shoulder head. This is the profile of the doll shown in Plate 17 (p. 31).

Stuffed kid upper arms would also be sewn to the body. Kid upper arms, as well as kid complete arms, normally have a gusset at the elbow allowing movement without tearing. The gussets were inverted at the elbow back, so when the arm was straight only the stitching showed but when the arm was bent the gusset itself was revealed. (The 'open' and 'closed' gusseting is shown in Plates 57 and 58, p. 81).

All the upper arms made of leather or fabric were sewn. Many were made in two halves with the seams down the front, approximately in line with the thumb, and down the back, approximately in line with the little finger.

The front of a kid arm in Plate 75 shows the seam, while the back of the arm in Plate 76 shows the seam and gusset. (These two illustrations are of the arm of the doll shown in Plate 18, p. 32.)

Moulded composition upper arms needed to be designed to fit bodies and their tops at the shoulder line were either ball shaped to fit into the body socket or cupped with a separate ball which fitted both into the arm and into the body.

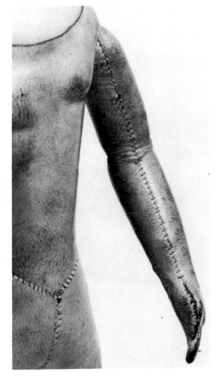

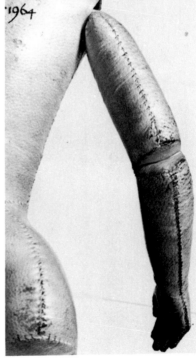

*Plate 75*

**Plate 76**

The arm of a Simon and Halbig adult doll in Plate 77 shows the whole arm with the arrangements made for the various parts to fit together. It is rare to find a composition upper arm with anything but a composition lower one. The elbow end of both the upper arm and the lower arm is a socket shape. Between the two ends is placed a separate ball allowing movement. Sometimes only one part of the arm will have a socket while its matching part will end in a ball shape.

Composition upper arms are cast and hollow, internally reinforced with a cross dowel and usually wood at the sockets. When made up and jointed the elastic stringing passes through an opening at the shoulder.

When the upper arm design may be described as simple, because its shape is basic and the number of materials used is few, the lower arm must be described as very complex. This part of the arm is often the only other visible area of a doll after the head and neck. Its design is a guide to the type of doll, its age and cost, the age of the person it represents and the skill and imagination of both the doll maker and the limb maker. Lower arms come in two forms, those with integral hands and those with separate hands. Again we will follow the changes in roughly date order, starting with the arm complete with the hand.

It must be remembered that head makers did not necessarily make limbs and as doll making became more industrialised, companies solely making limbs were founded. As many dolls were assembled by yet a third group of people, the same make of limbs could be used for different makes of head.

The design for arms, whether the complete arm or the divided arm, is quite complicated because the two arms of a doll must match but at the same time be opposites. The left arm must be the reverse of the right, the elbow must appear to bend correctly and the placing of the thumb must be in the right place on the hand.

The late 17th and early 18th century dolls had the arm and hand quite delicately designed, longer than normal and ending with graceful fingers and nails. Each finger is separate and the whole hand curves inwards.

The lower arms and hands in Plate 78 are made of wood which is covered with gesso, painted and varnished. These are the arms of the doll shown on the right of the Frontispiece.

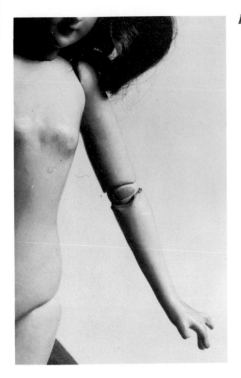

*Plate 77*

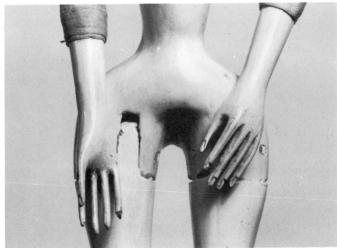

*Plate 78*

The lower arms of wood in Plate 79 have been carved and painted in the same manner and then covered with a fine kid to appear like and represent a pair of gloves. This is the arm of the doll shown in Plate 19 (p. 33).

*Plate 79*

During the 18th century, all kid lower arms were used. These were stuffed with sawdust or hair and appeared rounder and more realistic.

*Plate 80*

Sophie has all kid arms (Plate 80) which at one time were stuffed with sawdust but now they are almost flat due to an attack of woodworm which left a great many small holes. You will see that she has a separate thumb stitched to the kid which seems to be attached to the palm, but originally it would have appeared normal.

A fourth method of forming an 18th century doll's arm and hand was to use a flat piece of wood, carved crudely to resemble fingers and thumb. Even though there is an attempt to distinguish the thumb from the fingers, there is none of the quality carving and painting or attention to details, such as the nails.

The wooden hand of a wooden head and torso doll of about 1770 is shown in Plate 81. The body of this doll is shaped with card to give the impression of stays and the doll is dressed in red and white silk woven in the Spitalfields area of East London about 1760. However, the dress style is that of the early 1770s. The doll was made in England and stands 14½ins. tall.

*Plate 81*

Stuffed kid, of various colours other than flesh tints, was in common use throughout the 19th century. It is probable that by using a different colour of kid, the arms served the dual purpose or function of representing both arms and gloves.

Colour Plate 6 (p. 109) shows blue kid arms combined with a wax over composition head, a cloth body, glass eyes and a mohair wig. This doll is fashionably dressed for the period 1820-25. She was made in Germany and stands 13¾ins. tall. The wax of the head has greatly faded to become almost white.

*Plate 82*

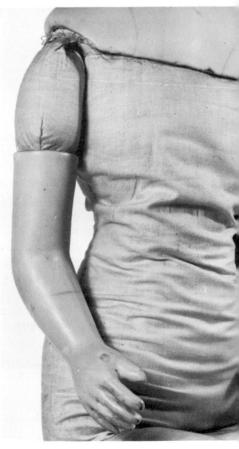

*Plate 83*

The sewing of the kid could reveal quite a lot about the skill of the maker. If you look again at Plates 75 and 76 (p. 101), these arms have a professional appearance with even stitches along the seams which run at the front and back. Sometimes the stitches are on the outside, as in Colour Plate 6, and at other times on the inside where the arms has been turned when sewn. On the other hand, there are some very crudely sewn arms showing the lack of expertise of the maker.

The brown kid arm in Plate 82 (p. 107) shows poor quality stitching. This arm also shows a hand with a thumb but only three fingers whereas Colour Plate 6 shows four fingers. This doll was made in Germany about 1825 and once belonged to Queen Mary, consort of George V.

By the time kid arms were used with the fashion dolls of the 1860s and 1870s (Plate 75, p. 101), they were formed over a padded wire frame and expertly designed with fine stitches and gussets. Occasionally these forms have been damaged by the wire protruding or in some cases, the wire going rusty thus staining the kid.

Except on rag dolls, cloth lower arms are quite rare. Cloth is not as durable as the other materials. Wax, on the other hand, makes good lower arms, although care must be taken not to damage it. Wax is only used for complete arms when used on all-in-one dolls and for lower arms, never for upper arms. It is cast in a mould like a wax head, generally hollow, though towards the fingers it may be solid. The hand is an integral part of the whole. These lower arms have holes along the top edge, reinforced with metal eyelets though which linen thread is passed to sew the arm to the cloth or kid upper arm, shown in Plate 48 (p. 71).

Occasionally glue is also used to hold the lower arm in place but more often when the lower arm is made of wax over composition. Such arms are made in the same manner as wax over composition heads with the composition moulded, then covered with a thin layer of wax. Like the heads, the wax on the arms is often crazed.

Plate 83 (p. 107) shows a wax over composition arm glued onto a cloth upper arm. (The head is shown in Plate 13, p. 28.)

Composition lower arms, as with composition upper arms, bodies and legs, are moulded, and after being rubbed down are painted and varnished. Many were designed with the hand as part of the whole but some, particularly on the larger sizes, had separate

*Colour Plate 6. Wax over composition shoulder head, with a cloth body, blue kid arms, glass eyes and a mohair wig. German, c.1820-25, height 13¾ins.*

hands. Generally the lower arm was straight in length and round in body tapering towards the wrist. The elbow end finished in one of two ways — either with a socket to take a separate ball which fitted both the lower and upper arms or with a round knob or ball. If the arm finished with the second method the knob had a hook embedded into it to take the elastic stringing. Please look again at Plate 77 (p. 103) which shows a composition arm.

Ball and Socket Jointing is the common term used when a separate ball is placed at the joint. While this method of jointing is normally seen cn larger dolls, it was often used for quite small dolls too. In common with all the other joints of a composition bodied doll, the immediate area of the joint is strengthened by wood and there is usually a wooden dowel across the inside of the limb.

If the hand is not part of the lower arm, then the arm must have a socket into which the hand fits at the wrist line. The hand will be designed with a knob at the wrist into which is embedded a hook for the elastic stringing. Generally composition lower arms are hollow and the elastic passes through them to the hooks in the hands. Should a composition lower arm be attached to a cloth

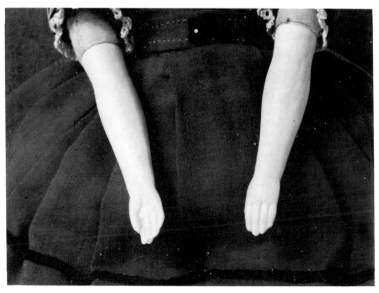

*Plate 84*

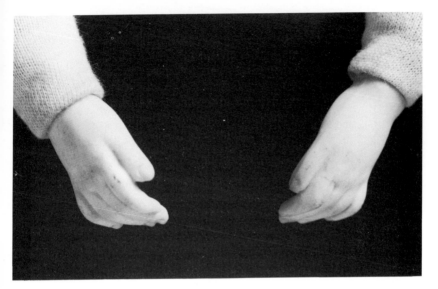

*Plate 85*

upper arm, it will have a ridge at the elbow round which is placed the cloth to be gathered and sewn in place in the same manner as a flange joint.

During the latter part of the 19th century and in the 20th century, wooden arms were occasionally produced to look and work like composition arms. These were hollow and had sockets at all the joints. After being carved, they were covered with thin gesso, then painted and varnished. The balls used in ball and socket jointing were always of wood, drilled with a hole through the centre for the elastic stringing and painted in the same manner.

Glazed china and bisque were in very common use to make lower arms.

The glazed china lower arms in Plate 84 are of the doll shown in Plate 27 (p. 48). Plate 85 illustrates the bisque lower arms on the doll body shown in Plate 64 (p. 87). The arms in both Plates 84 and 85 are sewn to the upper arms and have a ridge at the joint line. Glazed china and bisque could also be glued but sometimes they were combined with other forms of jointing such as gussets.

Plate 86 shows a bisque lower arm which is glued into kid. This part of the kid upper arm section is connected with a gusset. (The head is shown in Plate 15, p. 30.)

*Plate 86*

When celluloid was produced for lower arms it was generally as a replacement. It was moulded and jointed in the same way. Vinyl tends to be used only for the complete arm, though on recently made dolls, there is often an internal jointing like a metal framework allowing the different parts to move.

Plate 87 illustrates the vinyl arm of the New Active Sindy Ballerina. As the name suggests, this doll has limbs which can be moved although there is no obvious jointing except at the wrist and ankle. (This doll is shown in Plate 52, p. 76.)

*Plate 87*

# Hands

The design and construction of hands give very good pointers for dating dolls. As you look through the illustrations you will see that changes and improvements occurred. The type of material used, the cost of the doll and the artistry of the maker all affected the shape of the hands.

With wooden hands very definite changes can be seen, and as mass-production and cheapness increased the style deteriorated. The few dolls of the 17th century which have survived have kid covered hands (Plate 79, p. 104) and by the early 18th century, the hands were bare but of excellent design (Plate 78, p. 103). By the mid-18th century, crude hands were very evident regardless of the quality of the rest of the doll (Plates 73 and 81, pp. 99 and 106). Gradually throughout the 19th century, the carving deteriorated from separate fingers to lines carved in the wood to the crudest of all, hands that were just blunt ends (Plate 24, p. 41).

During the 18th century, kid was introduced for the making of hands which were quite elegant in shape following the long fingered pattern of the early wooden hands (Plate 80, p.105). By the early 19th century when coloured kid became fashionable, the hands could be of two types, either very well made and designed with a thumb and four fingers (Colour Plate 6, p. 109) or very crude with only three fingers (Plate 82, p. 107). The later fashion dolls of the 1860s onwards when kid was used had well defined hands in keeping with the rest of the doll (Plate 76, p. 101). Although these hands are from the French doll shown in Plate 18 (p. 32), good quality kid hands were not restricted to French dolls during this period.

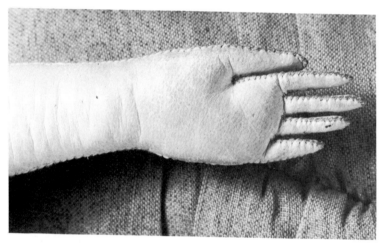

*Plate 88*

Plate 88 shows the kid right hand of the German doll in Plate 17 (p. 31). The hand has individual fingers and thumb, each carefully sewn and padded with kapok.

The use of kid had ceased by the 20th century. It was replaced by other materials such as bisque, composition and cloth. It would seem that the materials which could be moulded would produce the best styled hand. It happened in many cases but not in the majority. Rarely does one see separate fingers: either all four fingers and sometimes the thumb are together (Plate 84, p. 110) or the thumb, first and small fingers are separate and the middle two are together (Plate 70, p. 96). Good styling is not restricted to hands for adult dolls either (Plates 77 and 85, pp. 103 and 111) and some of the most expressive hands can be found on baby dolls (Plate 70, p. 96). Some of the cruder styling can be seen in Plates 27, 29 and 68 (pp. 48, 50 and 91). Most moulded hands curl slightly towards the palm but other styles are used, for example the fist (Plate 2, p. 17) and the star shape (Plate 4, p. 18).

Vinyl is slightly easier to mould with separate fingers which can be quite delicate (Plates 32 and 87, pp. 53 and 113) but baby hands tend to look lumpy (Plate 71, p. 97) as do those of modern bisque (Plate 67, p. 89).

When cloth was used to make hands, the thumb and fingers may only be indicated by rows of stitching (Plate 39, p. 61) but some makers did separate all but the centre two fingers.

The hands of the Lenci doll illustrated in in Plate 89 are made of felt and slightly padded. The thumb, first and small fingers are individually sewn but the two centre fingers are sewn along their outer edge and divided only by a row of stitches down the centre. (The head is shown in Plate 37, p. 59.)

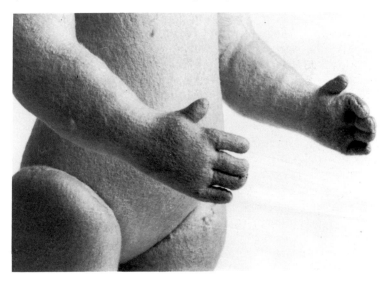

*Plate 89*

115

# Legs

Legs follow the same principles as those for arms. They are found to be either complete or divided at the knee, but rarely at the ankle. Almost all the dolls you will find will have a foot moulded as part of the lower leg.

Legs are proportionately longer and larger than the arms and, of course, added to the head and body give the overall height of the doll. As the majority of the leg went unseen when the doll was dressed, the finishing treatment of each part of the leg might be different, though care was usually taken with the design of the whole leg. Ankles were generally well shaped, chubby for a baby and trim for an adult doll, and most knees had some indication, though often it was to assist the movement rather than for looks. Thighs too were often well shaped and the better the design of the thigh, the easier it is to sit the doll.

## The Complete Leg

Like the complete arm, the complete leg is rarely found on early wooden dolls or late large ones, but is found on small wooden dolls. It is found on the all-in-one doll and on small jointed glazed china or bisque dolls or those designed to represent babies (Plates 2 and 62, pp. 17 and 84). Also like the arm, the greatest use of the complete leg appears when the limb is made of composition and later of vinyl. Such legs appear on those dolls designed to represent babies, bent limb, or young children, toddler. The legs should match the style of the arms and the body (Plates 69-70, pp. 95 and 96).

Where the design of the complete leg differs greatly from that of the complete arm is in the leg made of cloth. The head may be of any material but generally it is of wax, composition or the combination of wax over composition. The leg may be made from a single piece of cloth, shaped, sewn and stuffed to create the illusion of a leg and foot or it may be made of several pieces all sewn together before completing the leg. There can be a single seam running up the back of the leg or two seams running lengthwise up both the front and back, and sometimes the foot is made from another piece sewn on at the ankle. The foot may also be stitched to show the toes. After being stuffed, the top of the leg is sewn to the base of the body. Sometimes the legs just dangle and you may find that the toes point either inwards (→ ←) or outwards (← →) as well as straight ahead.

On rag dolls, of course, the legs may be part of the body but some do have separate legs, again sewn to the base of the body. In the case of felt dolls, such as the Lenci, the legs are also made of felt though they may be stiffened and slightly shaped indicating the knees with small dents.

Plate 90 shows a complete leg of cloth with a single seam running up the front and a single seam running up the back. This doll, which stands 14½ins tall, has a poured wax head and lower arms, with glass sleeping eyes operated by a wire through its body. The doll was presented to the Bethnal Green Museum in 1873 by a lady who stated that she had had the doll as a child and it was given to her in 1807.

*Plate 90*

Cloth, particularly if it has been stuffed with something liked by insects, may now be suffering the consequences of age and damage. You may find the legs are leaking sawdust or that they may have actual holes or tears. Patching will, in fact, increase the problem as it puts more strain on the material and every time a needle is stabbed into the cloth it damages the threads. One solution is to make a 'sock' covering of new cotton. This will hold the sawdust in place without further damage and it can be removed at any time if necessary. Sadly it is also possible that the original cloth is so badly damaged that replacement becomes necessary. In such cases, choose a cloth which closely matches the original and design the new limb following the pattern of the old one. This practice can be followed for the body and arms too. Be sure to keep the original pieces even when they are in a poor state.

Kid was also used to make complete legs, sometimes with gusseting at both the hips and knees. In many cases, the kid extended at the top to form part of the body; however, the feet were often of a separate piece sewn on at the ankle or heel line to give a better shape (Plates 59 and 100, pp. 81 and 124).

Details about the jointing and casting of the complete arm are discussed on pp. 94-98 and apply equally to the complete leg.

## The Divided Leg

Much of the information given on pages 98-112 under the section on the divided arm applies to the jointing of the divided leg.

If you again consider the Frontispiece showing the two early wooden dolls you will see that although both have divided legs with knee joints, the earlier (right) has been more carefully designed. The thigh and the calf are well shaped, rounded and feminine. In fact, they are so well designed, that when the legs are straight, the knee shape is produced and, but for the line, one would almost believe they are complete legs. The lower legs taper to form the ankles and the feet. On the later doll, the legs are rectangular blocks with edges rather than curves though some attempt has been made to indicate the calf and the tapering of the ankle. Also the final treatment of the legs is different with the earlier having paint-work to match the rest of the body and head, while the other has legs painted with one coat of matt white. Later on, no attempt was made to really shape the legs and finally the only areas to be painted were the feet (Plate 24, p. 41). The jointing of the legs is fully described within the jointing section of this chapter.

The divided leg need not have both the thigh and lower part of the same material, in fact many times they were different. It is always essential to remember that most dolls were designed to be dressed and, as with the arms, only those parts which would ultimately show needed any special treatment. In most cases this treatment was only given to the lower leg, for example a wooden body may have glazed china lower legs as well as a glazed china head and lower arms. When the body was made of cloth, the thigh was also made of cloth joined to the body by stitches at the top of the leg. Little shaping was achieved but sometimes two large knots of thread or a line of stitches were placed at the knee so it could bend more easily. The material used to make the lower leg was usually determined by the material used for the head.

Plate 91 (overleaf) illustrates wax over composition legs with cloth thighs and body. The head of this doll is also of wax over composition and is shown in Plate 13 (p. 28). Another illustration of this doll (Plate 56, p. 80) shows the line of stitches holding the legs to the body. In this case, the lower legs are glued to the base of the thigh.

Poured wax lower legs were usually sewn to the thighs using holes with eyelet reinforcements similar to the arms. Wax lower legs tended to stop at the knee line with little shape or indication of the knee itself.

The doll with the 'Gesland' body (Plate 64, p. 87) has well defined thighs matching the care taken to shape the rest of the body. Likewise its lower legs, made of bisque (Plate 92, overleaf), are well shaped. The upper edge of the leg has a flange ridge around which to gather the material from the thigh. The legs show a calf and a trim ankle but only a swelling for the knee.

Cloth is generally not used for the lower leg, although there are some German dolls with it, in particular those with a Ne Plus Ultra Patent Joint at the hips. In these cases, the kid of the thigh extends below the gusset at the knee and the cloth is sewn on at that point, as shown in Plate 93 (overleaf).

With the development of the composition body came the development of the composition divided leg which gave greater freedom of movement to the doll. There was the simple divided leg

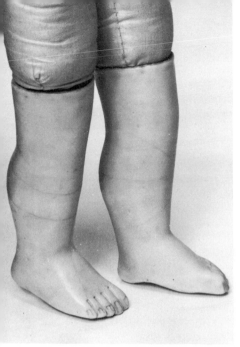

*Plate 91*

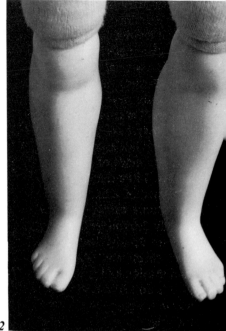

*Plate 92*

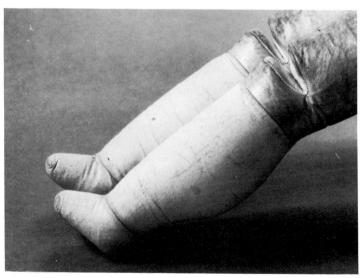

*Plate 93*

120

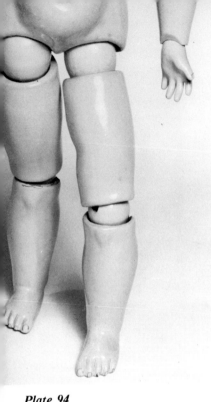

*Plate 94*

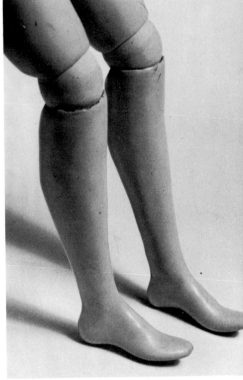

*Plate 95*

with the thigh having a knob at the top and a cup at the base and the lower leg having a knob at the top. There was the ball jointed leg with the thigh having a knob or separate ball at the top and a cup at its base and the lower leg having a cup at its top with a ball separating the two leg sections.

Initially the separate ball at the knee formed the knee with the two leg parts stopping short. However, as dress fashions changed and skirts shortened, it became necessary to adapt the shape of the lower leg. Thus the thigh became shorter, the ball was raised and the lower leg was designed to show the knee cap itself. By the late 1920s and 1930s this pattern became very exaggerated particularly on cheap dolls and as a result the leg did not bend at or around the knee but mid-way up the thigh.

Plate 94 shows a ball jointed leg of composition and Plate 95 a ball jointed adult leg of composition.

It is quite rare to find a separate foot other than those sewn on; however, there are some and these are discussed in Chapter 8. It is also very rare to find divided legs made of plastics and vinyl, though in some cases there is internal jointing to provide movement at the knee and ankle as for example the Sindy doll which has internal knee joints but an external swivel ankle joint held by a metal pin at the ankle.

## Feet

Wooden feet, thoughout the period we are covering, tended to be simply carved with little shaping of the ankles and no shaping of the toes. Usually feet were covered with stockings and shoes and such delicate carving was not necessary. Sophie's wooden feet (Plate 96) show the lack of carving. (See also Plate 24, p. 41.)

*Plate 96*

*Plate 97*

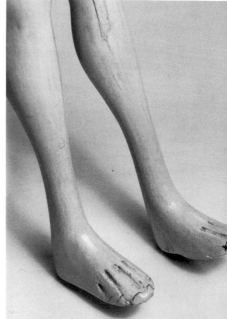

Occasionally of course, there were exceptions and the delicate treatment of the 1700 doll's feet follows the treatment given to the rest of her body.

The wooden feet (Plate 97) of the 1700 doll show the carving of the toes and ankle and the paintwork which matches the rest of the body. (See also Frontispiece, right.)

Like the hands, moulded materials allowed finer modelling as can be seen in Plates 91, 92 and 94 (pp. 120-1). Moulded feet can show the differences between the chubby baby foot (Plates 50 and 70, pp. 74 and 96) and the high arched narrow adult foot (Plate 95).

From the 1830s until about 1880, glazed china lower legs were

*Plate 98*

fashioned and painted to show stockings and shoes or boots. At first, the shoes were heelless but as the fashions changed the heel was introduced.

Plate 98 shows glazed china legs, painted near the top to show a garter and bow. The ankle and foot are also painted to show flat boots including the laces. Plate 27 (p. 48) shows much cruder feet which are also painted to show the garter and bow and the boots.

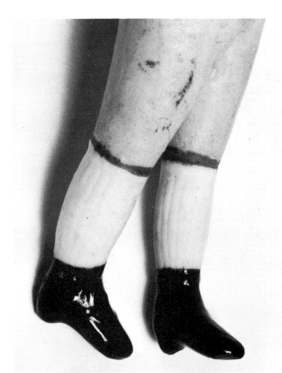

*Plate 99*

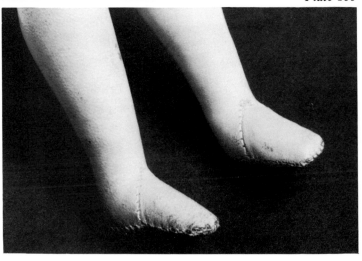

*Plate 100*

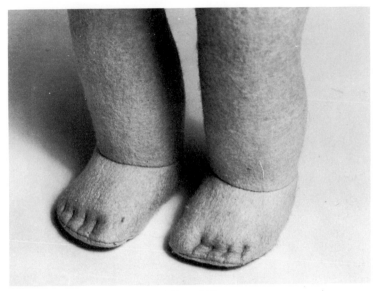

*Plate 101*

The bisque legs in Plate 99 have the lower part moulded and are painted to show ribbed stockings and heeled shoes. (The doll is shown in Plate 8, p. 23.)

Kid and cloth tends to be less shapely than the moulded materials. An example of kid feet is shown in Plate 100 in which seam lines may be seen joining the upper foot to the ankle and leg and the sole to the upper foot. (These are the feet of the doll shown in Plate 18, p. 32.)

The felt feet in Plate 101 are those of the Lenci doll. They show the seam joining the feet and legs at the ankles. The soles are flat and the toes are indicated by short rows of stitching.

## Jointing

The assembling of all the different parts of a doll to produce the whole is termed the Jointing. I have already made some reference to the jointing and you will have noticed that it does vary considerably depending upon the materials used for the head, body and limbs and on the style of the doll and its head.

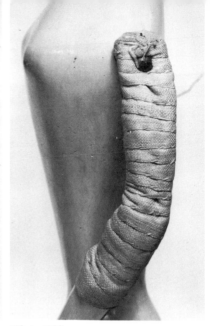

*Plate 102*          **Plate 103**

All-in-one dolls have no jointing whatsoever. Where such a doll, made of bisque or glazed china, has moving arms, the arms are attached to each other by a length of string or elastic running through the body.

Head and torso dolls of wood have different forms of jointing, one for the arms and another for the legs. On this type of doll, you will not find a complete wooden arm. The lower arm may be of wood, cloth or kid attached at the elbow level to linen which may be covered by the material of the dress worn. This upper arm may be sewn to the body with thread which passes through holes made in the side of the shoulder of the body. On the other hand, the upper arm may be simply nailed to the body. This attachment allows less movement than the first method, but as these dolls were to be dressed and admired and not actually played with, the movement of the arms was not so necessary.

Plate 102 shows the attachment of the upper arm by sewing it with thread through holes at the shoulder. (This is Sophie, Frontispiece, left.)

Plate 103 shows the attachment of the upper arm by nailing it to the shoulder. As you will see, it has been nailed two or three times during its life. (This is the doll on the right of the Frontispiece.)

The statements about the simplicity of the arm attachments seem to oppose the fact that the legs were well jointed. However, while the dolls were to be admired, they could be positioned to stand up or sit down, hence the need to provide some freedom for the legs. At this period during the 17th and 18th centuries, the legs had two sets of joints, one at the hip and the second at the knees. The hip line or bottom of the body was shaped at the front with two cut out lengths running upwards. Into these slits were placed the tongues retained at the top of the wooden legs. Metal or wooden pegs were then placed across the width of the hip securing the tongues in the slits and allowing them to pivot towards the front, as in the hip of the 1700 doll shown in Plate 104.

Likewise, slits were made in the base of the thigh block at the knee level into which the tongues at the top of the lower legs were placed and pinned allowing the knees to bend towards the back. Thus when the doll was stood up the legs hung straight down, but when the doll was placed in a seated position, the legs bent correctly at the hip and knees. The doll actually sat on the base of the body or its bottom and was quite stable.

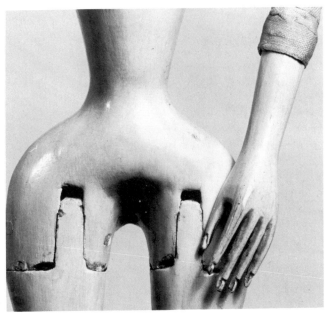

*Plate 104*

*Colour Plate 7.* "*Cedric*", *bisque socket head, with a jointed composition body, glass sleeping eyes and a mohair wig. Made by Simon and Halbig. German, c.1903, height 9ins.*

Plate 105 shows Sophie's hip with one leg bent into the sitting position. The knee joints of both dolls are well shown in the Frontispiece.

As the quality of these dolls decreased and when small ones were made, often the legs had no joints except at the hip line. During the latter part of the 19th century and in this century, all wooden dolls had wooden arms jointed at the shoulders, and depending on the size, at the elbows. The tongue and slit method was used in most cases but sometimes a ball was added at the shoulder to allow the arm to move sideways as well as forwards and backwards. When a wooden body was used in conjunction with a glazed china head and lower limbs, the same principle of the tongue and slit pinning was used.

Shoulder heads mounted on wooden bodies would be glued on and the body and limbs jointing was done as described above. It is quite rare to find shoulder heads on composition bodies. In such cases, they are either glued on or held by a metal disc in the head attached to metal wires and elastic in the body. This is very rare as the pressure required by elastic jointing is powerful and the assembler would run the risk of damage to the head by the disc.

*Plate 105*

One example of this type of jointing is that shown in Plate 50 (p. 74).

On the whole shoulder heads are mounted on cloth or kid bodies, regardless of the material used to make the limbs, though upper limbs are often the same material as the body. With a cloth body, stuffed with either sawdust or animal hair, the head is placed over the top seam and glued or sewn on. When glued, one might find that it is now brown with age, hard and cracking. If the head has come away, you must clear off all the old glue before attempting to reglue the head. However, if the head has the holes in the shoulder plate, it would be better to sew it on rather than use glue. The thread used for sewing on a head is linen, drawn tight enough to keep the head steady but loose enough not to cut into the cloth and tear it, and a heavy crochet cotton is recommended.

Wax shoulder heads, mounted either on a cloth or kid body, are attached in the same way — sewing through the holes being the more usual. The shoulder plate holes should be reinforced with metal eyelets which stop the linen thread from cutting into the wax.

A poured wax shoulder head which is sewn to the body is shown in Plate 106. The body bears the stamp of Mrs. Lucy Peck who was a maker, repairer and distributor of dolls in London from 1891 to 1921. This doll was made in England and stands 20ins. tall.

Cloth upper arms are sewn to the body at the shoulder and covered when the head is in place, whereas cloth upper legs are attached to the base of the body with a fine line of stitches which allow movement. Lower arms and legs are attached by the dictates of the material of which they are made. Wax ones are sewn on through the reinforced holes, but wood and china ones may have a slight ridge around the top over which the upper limb cloth is placed, gathered and stitched. Whole cloth or cloth and kid limbs are stitched where necessary.

Shoulder heads and swivel heads, when mounted on kid bodies, are sometimes placed inside the kid, glued onto the body with the edge of the kid glued to the plate. This often covers any marks which might be on the shoulder plate and I have seen the disastrous results of someone trying to raise the kid. The kid is very porous and the glue is firm. Any attempt at freeing the kid can result in tearing it. It is possible to lift the kid but this should be done by an expert to save damaging the doll. Nevertheless, the kid is usually

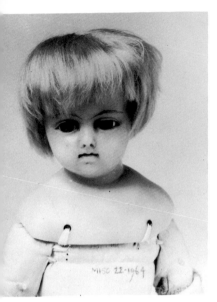

*Plate 106*

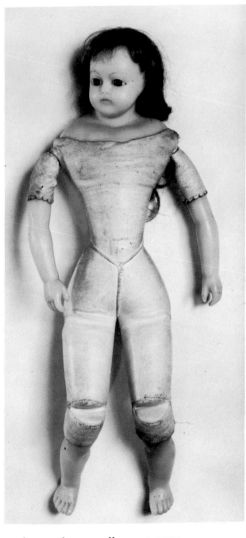

*Plate 107*

decoratively shaped into scallops to enhance the overall appearance of the doll.

Plate 107 shows a wax shoulder head mounted inside the upper edge of a kid body. This doll was made in England about 1860 and stands 16ins. tall.

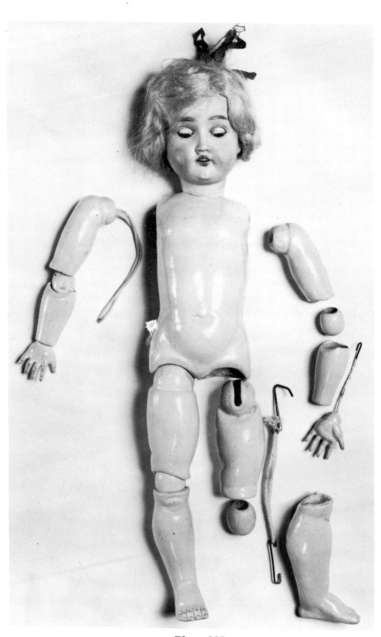

*Plate 108*

Socket heads are most often placed on the composition moulded bodies specifically designed for them. These bodies have sockets or cups to take the rounded neck base of the head and also the rounded ends of the limbs.

The partly dismantled doll in Plate 108 shows the stringing used for most bisque and composition dolls. Please refer to this 'exploded' illustration when working out how and if your doll is jointed this way. It is the standard method of jointing a socket head with a composition body, although some variations do occur.

The parts of the doll are held together with wire and elastic. The elastic is shirring or round elastic of varying thicknesses and strengths to cope with the size and weight of the doll. The head is strung to the legs and arms to each other. This is a very important point to remember, especially if your doll has elastic which is old and deteriorating. One careless move could result in the breaking of either the head or the legs or both. As already stated, all areas of the jointing except the head are strengthened because of the pressure from the elastic which must be tight enough to hold all the parts together.

Inside the head is placed a disc of wood or card, through which is placed a metal hook. At the top of each lower arm and leg is placed a metal hook or bar around which is also attached a hook. Sometimes the hook may be embedded into the knob and in the case of separate hands, it is embedded into the wrist. On large dolls, lengths of metal with a hook at each end are also used. To attach the head and the legs, two pieces of elastic of the appropriate length are cut and formed into two circles by stapling or knotting the ends together. Each circle is placed into the hook of the lower leg, passed through the ball at the knee (if a ball is used) into the thigh and up into the body to be attached to the hook from the head. If the doll is large, straight lengths of metal, or sometimes a triangle, with a hook at each end, are used. These are attached to the elastic in the body and then to the head hook.

Arms are attached to each other and use a single circle of elastic stretching from the hand or lower limb on one side, through the upper arm and body to the hook on the other arm. Colour Plate 7 (p. 128) shows a composition body assembled with a bisque socket head. This doll, known as "Cedric", was made by the German firm Simon and Halbig and bought from Whiteley's of London in 1903.

He is wearing a sailor suit, a popular outfit for children at the time, but he has a number of different outfits which are housed in a saratoga trunk.

Some crude, cheap dolls will have the elastic pegged into a hole at the top of each limb. The difficulty with this form of jointing

*Plate 109*

comes when the elastic begins to deteriorate and all the pieces become loose. Be very careful when handling a doll with perished elastic as the parts will sometimes fall off and they are breakable. Plate 109 shows an all bisque doll with elastic stringing simply pegged and knotted into place.

Flange joints consist of a ridge on the head and limbs around which are placed the material of the body. If the body is cloth, then the cloth is gathered, tightened and sewn to the ridge. Modern vinyl dolls often use the flange joint with all the area to be jointed specially designed so they slot together easily.

*Plate 110*

*Plate 111*

Plates 110 and 111 show the top of the leg showing the ridge and a view inside the lower body of the same doll to show the leg in position. This is the doll shown in Plate 23 (p. 38) and you will notice that the areas which are normally not seen have not been cleared of the waste after the moulding was completed.

What we have been discussing are the most commonly found methods of jointing and most dolls, regardless of head, limb and body materials will be jointed by one of these methods. However, there are other forms of jointing, some of which are known to have been patented. The following examples are just a few of these many types but they are the ones you are most likely to come across.

For example, ball jointing was in use during the 18th century but generally on dolls which were articulated artists' models. This method, using wood, had limbs ending in knobs but fitting together almost the same way as the tongue and slit method. The joint was more mobile and smoother; it allowed considerable freedom for positioning and today you can still buy this type of model.

During the early years of the 19th century, German makers produced a variation on the Dutch doll which had a wooden shoulder head and wooden lower arms and legs with a well designed stuffed kid body. The joints used bands of red or blue leather which were glued to both the body and the limb allowing movement without proper jointing. Such dolls are sometimes known as Sonneberg dolls.

During the 19th century, a number of makers patented special joints to create a particular movement or look. For example, Charles Motschmann of Germany in the 1850s developed a 'floating' joint system which replaced the upper arms, upper legs and the centre torso with tubes of cloth, while the chest, pelvis, and lower arms and legs remained in a harder material — composition, wood or ceramic. He also formed an unusual way of attaching the hands and feet so they remained quite loose, though not all his dolls had these parts as separate items.

Plate 112 shows a Motschmann doll with a composition head and glass eyes. The head, the hands and the feet are all attached by means of a small hook and bar and each is quite loose though there is no danger of them falling off. Within the torso is a small wood and paper bellows which surprisingly still works sometimes. With this type of bellows, the paper dries and cracks forming tiny holes and of course where there are holes, no sound is produced. Plate 113 shows the legs and feet of the Motschmann doll in detail.

With the commonly called 'Gesland' body, the name is found stamped on some doll bodies of the type, the body is a framework of metal swivel joints found at the shoulders, elbows, wrists, waist,

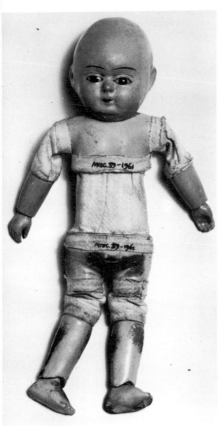

*Plate 112*

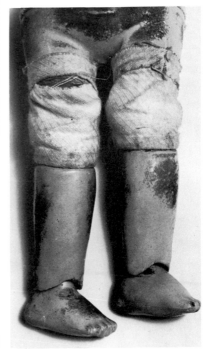

*Plate 113*

137

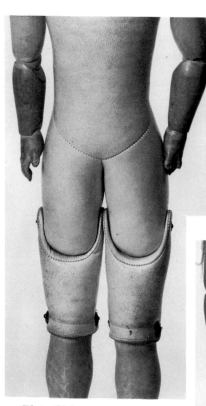

*Plate 114*

*Plate 115*

138

hips and knees. This framework was carefully padded with cotton wool bound with thread and the whole given an outer covering of cotton stockinet. The hands, head and lower legs, generally all made of bisque, were added to the framework. (See Plate 64, p. 87.)

In 1883 an American, Sarah Robinson, patented a method of jointing called grandly the Ne Plus Ultra Patent Joint. The principle was that the lower body extended to form the upper thigh of each leg to which the upper legs were then pinned. The top of the upper leg formed a U shape while the bottom was rounded to fit into the U shape of the lower leg, to become the knee. The knee joint was replaced later by another American patent of 1896 taken out by Charles Fausel. This joint, called the Universal, allowed a smoother movement where the knob of the lower leg moved freely with the cup of the thigh, and was held in place by a rivet through both.

Plate 114 shows the hip joint of a large Armand Marseille doll with a shoulder head. This shows the Ne Plus Ultra Patent Joint, and the Universal joint at the knee. Plate 115 shows the back view.

# Chapter 5
## Facial Features

As dolls were designed to be representations of human beings, their heads were designed to show facial features. That is to say, the head shows two eyes, a nose and a mouth, set upon the simulated bone structure of the forehead, brows, cheeks, jaw and chin of the face. Occasionally ears were also included.

The facial features were set out to be a pleasing sight to the eye of the beholder though sometimes due to colour changes, cracks, age and even changes in fashion, the faces may not have the pleasurable countenance for us that they did for their original owners.

The faces were stylised, some more than others, and reflected the desired fashionable look of the day as a Sindy doll represents the teenage look of the 1960s and 1970s. Most faces also showed a specific age of person, be it baby, child, teenager or adult. The majority, however, other than those of babies, were female rather than male. Few dolls of men or boys were produced, except those representing known people, dolls' house dolls where family life was portrayed, and the odd character doll which in some cases has the look of a caricature. From the turn of the century, more 'boy' dolls have been introduced and the rare 'man' such as G.I. Joe, or Action Man as he is known as in England.

Just why this should be so is not wholly understood but as the dolls were initially intended to be dressed, female attire is more flamboyant and more numerous. It must also be assumed that it was because girls or young women were the people who played with dolls, though this is not strictly true. The emphasis may have changed in recent years as at one time girls were required to learn housewifery, sewing and child care and dolls played their part by being used as manikins for the results, skilled or otherwise, produced by little fingers. There still remains today the adult concept that dolls are 'girls' toys and boys should play with other types of toys such as vehicles and soldiers. In my own experience, I have found while most young children copy their mothers in many ways and all make use of some form of comfort toy which is usually soft and cuddly, boys under the age of five tend to be happier finding out how a doll was made or how it works than nursing it or dressing it.

The facial characteristics of a doll must consist of the basic shape of the face, the type of eye which has been placed upon the face and the design of the mouth. I am going to discuss these three characteristics in greater detail as together they give the initial information about your doll and its age.

## The Shape of the Face

When you read any books or magazines about aids for beauty, the authors tend to refer first to the four face shapes. These are round, long, square and heart shaped. Surprisingly perhaps, dolls also follow these four shapes which are more pronounced on heads representing adults than on children. In general, this happens with human faces too.

The human face is created by the bone structure of the forehead, the cheeks and the jaw. A doll's face is created by illusion, it is an artist's impression only. There is no substructure and the maker tends to reflect the fashionable face of his day. Of course, the material with which he works influences the final appearance as some materials, such as china, lend themselves more easily to modelling than others, such as wood.

Wooden dolls, regardless of when they were made, have rather round faces, flat in appearance. The heads were created from a block of wood turned on a lathe and the only additional carving was done around the eyes, the nose and the mouth. Their adult looks were created by careful painting of the facial features and one can see as the painting became cruder that the look became more child-like. Please see the doll on the right of the Frontispiece and Plate 11 (p. 26).

Composition heads tend to be round, even bordering on square,with quite full areas either side of the chin. This seems to be the face shape favoured by German makers, regardless of the material used. However, when making a composition head, the prepared material is pressed into moulds and not easily shaped to show a 'fine boned' face. When such a head had a moulded hair style (see Plate 17, p. 31), the illusion of the adult face is often in the hair and delicate paintwork of the facial features rather than in the shape of the face.

Likewise with wax and wax over composition heads, it often appears that no attempt has been made to create an adult face. Many of these heads seem to adapt to whatever clothing the doll wears. Perhaps this is the art of doll making.

When makers used glazed china or bisque, there was more licence to create different facial types. Unlike wax, a balance did not need to be struck between durability and fragile casting. As I have said before, most doll making using china was done by companies already producing other items, such as tea sets, and figurines, and the knowledge gained in the other fields was applied to the doll making.

Makers could make definite distinctions between adult and children's faces. During the mid-19th century, when the use of glazed china was at its height, it was the adult face that was popular along with their elaborate hair styles. By the 1860s when the French fashion dolls made their appearance, the adult face was kept although occasionally there were some amusing results. One maker, Jules Nicholas Steiner of Paris, produced some very fine examples of adult dolls which were beautifully attired in the latest fashions. However, this maker was also very keen on the mechanical side and created walking and talking dolls. Some of his creations glide along looking as if they had been lifted from a fashion magazine while at the same time screaming 'mama' at you.

Plate 116 shows a French fashion doll's swivel head, made of bisque and marked FG. If you compare this head with that in Plate 17 (p. 31), you will see that it is much thinner along the jaw line. The head in Plate 116 was probably made by Gaultier of France, who was a maker of porcelain doll heads and parts from 1860 to after 1916. The head is of the doll shown in Plate 64 (p. 87).

The German socket head in Plate 117 is made of bisque. This head has a heart shaped face which is quite small and was made by Simon and Halbig about 1905. The body designed for it is slender and lithe looking (Plates 46-47, p. 70).

The adult face gradually gave way in popularity to the child face, then to the baby face. There were attempts to create faces that showed new born babies, year old babies and children ranging in age from two to fifteen.

*Plate 116*

*Plate 117*

143

The child face tends to be roundish, with a cheerful countenance and now often termed 'pretty'. Colour Plate 8 is an example of the child face. Its bisque socket head and jointed composition body were made in Germany about 1923 and it stands 14ins. tall. This is also an example of the gradual lowering of quality of manufacture which began after the First World War. Most makers found that they had several styles of head and face that proved popular and they continued to make them over a good number of years. For example, the 390 mould by Armand Marseille continued for about thirty years. After all, dolls were made to be bought, played with and admired and as businessmen with an eye to the trade, makers designed what the market would purchase. This principle still exists and dolls, such as a Sindy, have been in production for many years. There is always the drive to create an evermore natural and human-like doll and face. Commonly termed 'character', these developments are discussed separately.

It is not always possible to decide whether a doll has an adult or child face and when the body has one of those equally undefined shapes, the problem is increased. If the original clothes exist, they will give an indication of the age of the person represented. However, clothes also indicate the likes and dislikes of the original owner, and in some cases their ability to design and make clothes. If you have a doll with no clothing, then you must decide whether your doll is an adult or a child or even a baby. This is by no means an easy decision in every case.

Baby dolls are usually the easiest to recognise as they have different head shapes as well as body shapes. Likewise a lady doll may have a definite body shape with a bosom, narrow waist and wide hips. It is in the apparently vast middle range where the bodies seem to be of a standard shape and the heads of a standard design that most dolls seem to lie. As I have said, you as the owner must make the decision *if* you wish to dress your doll. The best advice I can give is to form an idea of what styles of clothes you like, seek examples of your doll in museums and books and then look at references for clothing. There are a number of good books which show the styles and also have instructions on how to make them. Do not forget that the undergarments are as important as the outer ones and that it is better to have clothing of a design contemporary with your doll. Remember that man-made fabrics are a recent

*Colour Plate 8.*
Bisque socket head,
with a jointed
composition body,
glass sleeping eyes
and a mohair wig.
German, c.1923,
height 14ins.

innovation and it is easy to obtain fine cottons, wools and silk although they may be a little more expensive.

# Face Colouring and Decoration

All finished doll heads and faces bear some form of colouring. As the majority represent Europeans, the basic colour fluctuates from white to shades of pink. Where other races are depicted, the colour varies from beige to very dark brown depending on the race represented.

Wooden dolls will have either an off-white or a pink complexion, though the colour may have changed because of the use of varnish which tends to yellow with age. If you compare the dolls in the Frontispiece, you will notice that Sophie has a very pink face. Early composition heads tend to be very pale with just a hint of pink. However, those heads which have been liberally varnished are usually quite yellow now. 20th century composition heads have normally quite dark complexions, almost as if they were wearing heavy make-up.

Wax and wax over composition heads vary between being pale pink to a dark purplish pink. Wax is very susceptible to fading in strong sunlight and some heads are bleached almost white. You can check if this has happened by looking under the hair line or at the lower limbs if these are made of the same material as the head. Where the wax has been covered, little fading occurs. There is no way of reclaiming the colour once the wax has faded but by careful and skilful cosmetic treatment it is possible to remove some of the deathly pallor. Such treatment should only be undertaken by an expert or under their guidance.

The basic colour of glazed china and bisque is chalk white. It is the top glaze which determines the final complexion. If you study Colour Plate 1 (p. 19), showing the glazed china heads, you will see that the colour can be white or pink. The majority in fact are white. On the other hand, while bisque heads can also be white and pink, the majority are pink. On the rare occasions stoneware is used for doll heads, the colour is in the material itself and it is usually a rather muddy pink.

Celluloid is another of the materials which is susceptible to fading unless it has been painted on the outside surface. Present day vinyls normally vary between the pale cream to the dark pink. As yet really not enough time has elapsed to see if there are any major colour changes in this material due to age. However, some of the hard vinyls made in the 1950s are now showing signs of fading. Really the only materials which do not appear to fade are those ceramics which are fired in a kiln.

The main facial feature decoration on each doll's face is a bright spot of colour on each cheek. Round in shape, the cheek spots vary in colour from bright pink to red, most dramatically seen on the white glazed china faces where the red often matches that used for the lips. On materials susceptible to fading, the cheek spots may also have disappeared. On wax heads, this colour was usually applied onto the surface and has either faded or been rubbed away. It is possible to give some delicate cosmetic treatment to restore it by choosing a good quality powered rouge of an appropriate colour. By using a little of the rouge on your finger gently rub it onto the surface, in a circular motion until the colour is right and the shape is a circle. In a few cases on cheap wax heads, the colour has been achieved by a stencil. It is not possible to replace the stencilled colour but if cheek spots are needed for the appearance of the doll, apply rouge in the manner just described.

The second main facial feature decoration is the painting of the lips. Generally a definite red, the colour can vary from pink to purple. Again the colour may be affected by age, fading and being rubbed off. On the whole, however, lip colour survives.

The shaping of the mouth is described later but the application of colour to the mouth has a much greater effect on the overall appearance of the face than the shaping. By a line here or a curve there, the whole facial expression can be altered. Great emphasis was placed on a 'cupid's bow' shape, well defined points on the upper lip and a generous swell in the lower lip. It must be remembered that all the decoration of facial features was done by hand. As such no two dolls are completely identical. Each will have its own individual traits and characteristics.

The painting of the nose was restricted to the painting of a red dot in each nostril. The majority of dolls have these dots unless they were very cheap ones or had only a painted circle to indicate the nose itself.

The painting around dolls' eyes was very delicate. Again it was by hand and the facial expression could be changed completely by a mere slip of the paint brush. Of course, some makers actively used the painting of the eyes to form the character of their doll and the best example is the smouldering look achieved by the Lenci factory.

On the 1680 wooden doll (Plate 19, p. 33), the painting of the eyebrows and upper lashes was the same. It consisted of single arched black lines with short black strokes rising at right angles from the lines. There were no lower lashes. The eyebrows and lashes of the 1700 (Plate 121, p. 153) are treated in a slightly different manner. The brows are formed from single arched black lines criss-crossed with short black strokes. Black strokes are also used around the eyes to show both upper and lower lashes. Sophie (Plate 122, p. 154), on the other hand, has eyebrows which are still arched black lines but the short strokes have been replaced by black dots. These are slightly wider than the lines so they appear both above and below the lines. Black dots are also used around each eye to indicate the upper and lower lashes. By the late 19th century, solid and usually straight lines were used for both the eyebrows and the upper lashes. There were no lower lashes and sometimes the painting on these wooden dolls was so basic that the facial expression looks very stern. Red dots, still used in theatrical make-up to differentiate the eyes from the nose, were sometimes used. The 1700 doll (Plate 121, p. 153) has red dots, both on the inner and outer edges of its eyes.

Composition heads had solid brow and upper lash lines and occasionally red dots. The colour, however, was not always black, in fact sometimes it was quite a light brown. Wax over composition heads tend to have eyebrows which have been painted with several very thin lines rather than one solid line and they look more realistic. Sometimes the painting is under the wax, probably done onto the composition base, sometimes it is drawn onto the wax and sometimes it is stencilled directly onto the wax. Occasionally, both upper and lower lashes were indicated by short straight strokes, and red dots are shown.

Wax heads show similar paintwork but several makers, such as Pierotti, inserted human hair into the wax both for the eyebrows and the lashes. The colour of the hair matched that used on the head. See the illustration of Lord Roberts (Plate 163, p. 194).

With the moulding of doll heads, more attention was given to the ridges around the eyes and many dolls had a crease just above the eye socket. This was not normally painted, but on some glazed china heads the crease was painted, usually a pinkish beige colour, and not moulded. Glazed china heads had solid lines for the brows and the upper lashes and the red dots but no lower lashes.

French bisque doll heads had feathered brows and long sweeping strokes for the upper and lower lashes, with the lower ones often very long between ¼in. and ⅜in. By also using the red dots, the final result was that the eyes appeared much larger.

Early German bisque heads were painted as were the glazed china ones. From about 1870 onwards, the brows the lashes were treated in the same manner as French bisque heads but with shorter lower lashes. With the advent of the sleeping eye, fur or hair lashes were attached to the eye itself, but the painted lashes remained. Occasionally strips of fur or hair were also glued over the painted brows. The painting of celluloid and early plastic doll heads followed the same methods as the German bisque heads but modern vinyl heads normally have only upper lashes.

There is one further painting exercise which only occurs on early wooden faces, namely 'patches'. Patches had been used by ladies to cover the ravishes of diseases such as smallpox and gradually they became part of the fashionable make-up whether one had scars or not. Many were the simple circles such as those on the 1680 doll (Plate 19, p. 33) but sometimes they were quite outlandish as one record of the time recalls a lady with a patch shaped like a stagecoach with a team of horses.

One facial feature decoration, and the only one which is not painted, is the dimple. Although chins were always well defined, few early dolls had this particular decoration. Most bisque dolls had a chin dimple, a round indentation in the centre of the chin. However, dimples in the cheeks are rarely found on any doll other than character dolls.

# Eyes

When you first look at a doll's face, the most outstanding feature is the eyes which seem to contain the very life of the doll. The treatment afforded the eyes varies considerably and it is one of the best indications of the date as well as the character of the doll. Eyes bring life and expression to a doll's face, whether they appear happy, sad or cross. The eyes can also indicate the original cost, not the actual price, but whether it was an expensive doll or not.

Throughout the last three hundred years, eyes changed in design and shape, changes were made in how they were shown and various inventions and patents were developed to increase the natural or realistic look of the eyes. The main types discussed here follow in a rough chronological order, though some types such as the painted eye are still used today.

## The Painted Eye

The idea of painting the eye onto the surface of the head has been in use throughout the period we are covering, and the treatment varies with the crudeness of the doll and the carving or modelling. However, the shape of the iris is usually three-quarters of a circle with the top cut square by the line of the upper lid. Sometimes the colour is two-toned, brown with a black pupil, and later blue with a black pupil. Painted pupilless eyes generally indicate a later date and smaller head.

If you study Plate 19 (p. 33) of the 1680 doll, you will see that the eyes are painted on the top of the finishing coat of paint. These eyes are well defined, near black in colour and highlighted with two white dots at the top of each. The treatment of the lids, lashes and eyebrows is also important and on this example, the lower lid remains unpainted and is only indicated by a slight swell in the carving of the wood. The arch of the eyebrow and the almost exaggerated slope of the upper lid are formed by a single line criss-crossed by a set of very small fine lines. This method of painting continued through most of the 18th century to be replaced by dots, and then solid lines which were sometimes feathered. If you look again at Plate 24 (p. 41), you will see how much the treatment of the eyes had deteriorated. With this example, the iris is painted blue but the black pupils are unevenly placed and there has been no attempt at carving the shape of the eye.

Painted eyes were not confined to wooden dolls, but appeared on all materials. The eyes of the composition doll shown in Plate 12 (p. 27) have white triangles painted on either side of the iris. This treatment was not constant and tends not to have been used on cheap dolls. If you also look at Colour Plate 1 and Plate 17 (pp. 19 and 31), you will see the use of the straightforward painted eye on both glazed china heads and bisque heads.

Painted eyes tend to stare to the front. In the 1920s, however, the side glancing eye was introduced. This treatment was most successfully used on the French cloth dolls, commonly called Bed dolls, and used by ladies as room ornaments, and on the dolls created by the Italian firm of Lenci.

Plate 118 shows an example of side glancing eyes. These are the eyes of the doll shown in Plate 38 (p. 60).

The side glancing eyes of the Lenci doll in Plate 119 make the doll look rather sullen although the maker's intention was to design dolls which showed a child's innocence.

*Plate 118*

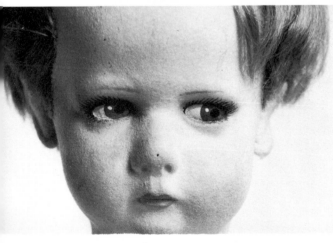

*Plate 119*

Modern vinyl dolls often have painted eyes which are sometimes over large and exaggerated. The eyes of the Sindy doll shown in Plate 52 (p. 76) are painted, though of a more normal size.

A slight variation on the painted eye is commonly called the 'intaglio' eye. This type of eye has been carved or moulded, in the case of china heads, inwards so that it actually appears convex though in fact concave. This treatment gives a depth to the eyes and was used extensively on character heads which are discussed elsewhere. Generally intaglio eyes are highlighted by a white dot on the iris.

Plate 120 shows the intaglio eyes of a character baby doll produced by Gebruder Heubach about 1910. The whole countenance of this doll is that of a happy infant and the eyes also seem to be smiling. The whole doll is shown in Plate 50 (p. 74).

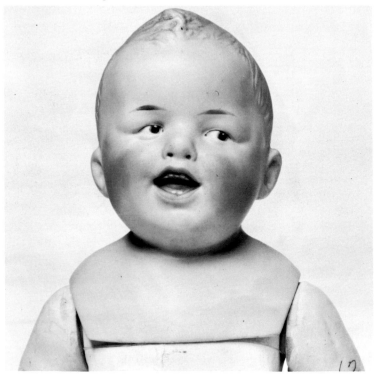

*Plate 120*

# The Glass Eye

The second common eye for dolls was the glass eye. There are three main categories of dolls with glass eyes and the first represents, in general, 18th century dolls of wood. The second category has hollow heads with the eyes placed inside and held in a rigid position while the third has eyes which are placed inside the head but move. From the 18th century onwards, doll heads of all materials could have glass eyes, with the notable exception of glazed china heads which had, until the latter part of the 19th century, painted eyes.

Plate 121 shows the glass eyes of the doll on the right of the Frontispiece. After the head had been turned from a solid block of wood, the eye sockets were cut out in the shape of a lozenge. The eye, usually pupilless with white triangles on either side and made of enamelled glass, was inserted into the prepared socket from the front. Throughout the 18th century, the iris was dark brown to black in colour, though it did vary in shape and size. This doll has very large irises covering almost the entire surface. The treatment of the lashes and brows shows that they are created by definite lines.

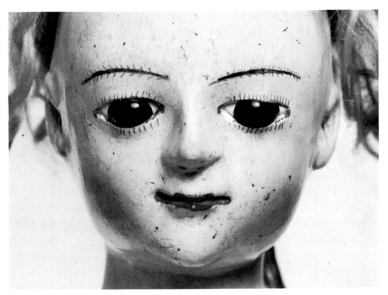

*Plate 121*

*Plate 122*

Plate 122 shows the glass eyes of Sophie. These eyes are also formed from enamelled glass and are placed onto the head in the same manner. However, the irises and the whites are more evenly distributed. The treatment of the lashes and brows is also different as these are now created by small dots rather than lines.

This form of enamelled glass lozenge-shaped eye was also found on some 18th century wax dolls, as seen in Colour Plate 5 (p. 92). Solid wax heads had glass eyes but generally they were beads either pinned to the head or set into the head by slightly warming the wax and pushing the bead on, to be held when the wax hardened again, or by using a small bit of molten wax between the bead and the head and allowing it to harden.

The eyes found in the 19th century heads look very much the same as those of the earlier century, though their construction and insertion were quite different. As discussed in Chapter 1, the manu-facture of the heads changed with the use of different materials and many heads were in fact hollow. Likewise, the manufacture of the eyes changed and they became blown glass irises, with or without the whites. Some of the eyes were quite plain just with the single colour iris and a black pupil; others, however, had what one might call 'paperweight' eyes, with the irises having drawn white threads through them to give a depth of colour and luminosity. Blown eyes were round, slightly flat in the front and coming to a point at the back. Some makers did produce very bulbous eyes, such as the Jumeau firm, and such eyes have become one of the main characteristics of their dolls. Colour Plate 9 (p. 164) shows a big Jumeau doll with its large bulbous blown glass eyes.

When a mould was designed, eye sockets were indicated and upon completion of the moulding of the head, the sockets were cut out. The placement of the eyes into the head was one of the last jobs to be done and followed the painting and final decoration of the head. The eyes were placed individually into the sockets from inside the head and held in place with a plaster mixture if the head was composition, glazed china or bisque, or wax if the head was made of wax. Because of their porous nature, the plaster mixture adheres very well to the composition and likewise, the wax to the wax. However, with glazed china and bisque, it is easy to push the eyes and their holding blocks out of alignment or dislodge them completely. The eyes placed in shoulder heads were inserted by going up through the hollow neck. This method was generally impossible to do on socket heads so these heads have a large hole in the crown which would eventually be covered by a cork or cardboard pate.

Plate 123 shows glass eyes within a wax over composition head, which is of German origin and dated between 1820 and 1825. These eyes have rather a pop-eyed stare. These eyes are similar to those of the doll shown in Colour Plate 6 (p. 109).

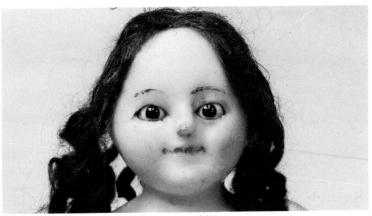

*Plate 123*

Plate 124 shows glass eyes within a wax head. These belong to the doll shown in Plate 10 (p. 25).

An example of glass eyes within a bisque head is illustrated in Plate 125. These eyes belong to the doll shown in Plate 116 (p. 143).

*Plate 124*

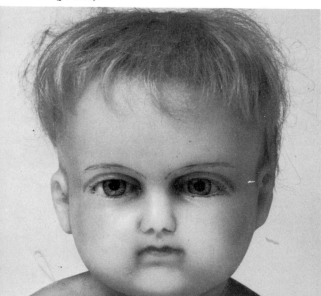

*Plate 125*

# The Sleeping Eye

Over the years, the eyes were changed both in colour and shape and many of the static eyes tended to give dolls a rather surprised, pop-eyes stare. It was perhaps the drive to create a more natural, human-like quality that gave the makers the inspiration to experiment with new forms of eyes and eye movements, thus creating the sleeping eyes in all their variations.

The first attempt at a sleeping eye mechanism was to operate manually the movement of the eyes. The eyes themselves were glass and linked at the back by a bar of metal or wood, usually embedded in plaster. To the link bar was attached a length of metal to form a rod. When the eyes were placed into the doll's head, they were held by a knob of plaster at each side. The freedom of movement was achieved by first coating the eyes with a greasy substance such as lard or vaseline. While the plaster hardened, the eyes remained static but the grease did not adhere to the plaster. Once the plaster had set, the grease could be removed and the eyes then moved freely within two cups of plaster each placed in the area behind the temple. To add to the freedom of the movement and also to provide an eyelid when closed, there was usually a coating of wax on the glass.

When the head, now complete with its eyes, was placed on a body, the metal rod was pushed through the body to protrude at the hip line, between the legs or in the thigh of one leg. To operate the eyes, you merely pushed or pulled the rod, gently of course!

Plates 126 and 127 (overleaf) show the rod protruding from the body of a doll with a poured wax head, and the glass eyes which it operates. This is the doll described on p. 117 with Plate 90.

This method was used on glazed china, early bisque and composition heads, but to a much greater degree on wax or wax over composition heads. It was safer for these heads which would not stand up to the force of a lead weight movement.

The second eye movement, which became the commonest and whose general principle is still used today, has the simple action of a moving weight or counter balance. The eyes are mounted in the heads as before and linked by a metal bar. To this bar, attached at right angles, is a short rod with a weight at the other end. This weight, originally a lump of lead, is slightly heavier than the total weight of the eyes and bars. When the head is in an upright

157

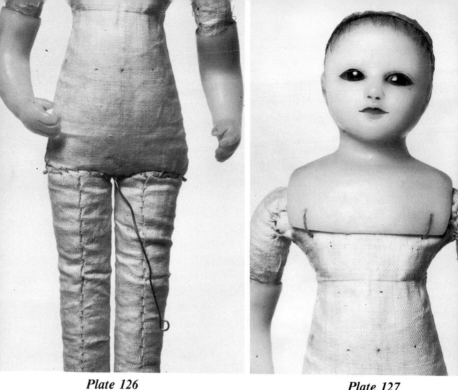

Plate 126

Plate 127

position, the weight hangs straight down reaching about the chin level and when the head is placed on its back in a sleeping position, the weight moves towards the back of the head forcing the eyes to move down so they appear to be closed. This is almost an optical illusion because the relationship between the weight and the eyes has not changed and in fact the weight is still hanging straight down. What has happened is that the head has turned a quarter circle in relation to the eyes.

To stop the movement going any further (for example a complete circle if the head is turned upside down) there is a small block of material, usually cork or wood, placed on the inside of the head between the eyes behind the bridge of the nose. This block prevents the linking bar travelling any further than a given amount.

There is also sometimes a small pad behind the mouth area to stop the weight knocking the face front. You will also notice on many bisque heads two small holes in the back of the head. These holes were used only when the head, or complete doll, was in transit. In order to keep the eye weight steady, a string or wire was passed through one hole, around the rod, through the second hole and tied on the outside. All that was needed to free the sleeping eye mechanism was to cut the end knot.

Plate 128 shows a sleeping eye mechanism. This set of eyes are of metal with glass eyes.

The sleeping eye mechanism was used for glass, metal and plastic eyes but over the last century many new ideas were tried out. For example, Jules Nicholas Steiner of Paris patented in 1880 a lever movement with a similar action to the original rod one except that the lever protruded at the side of the head. Also attempts were made to keep the eye static while the lids closed over them. None of these ideas proved popular as they were unsightly, costly or just not efficient.

Plate 129 shows the profile of a Steiner doll with the lever protruding from the head.

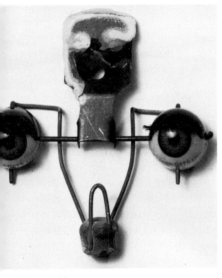

*Plate 128*

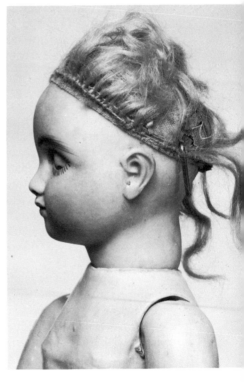

*Plate 129*

Improvements, however, were adopted in the counter balance mechanism. The major one was the 'flirting' eye. This was a side glancing as well as sleeping eye and there were two varieties. One was controlled by a lever which protruded from the back of the head. It could be switched to shift the position of the linking bar so that the eyes could look to the left or right as well as to the front. The sleeping mechanism remained the same. A second improvement, though not as satisfactory, used a rod, which, while attached to the linking bar, was not rigid so that the weight could be swung not only backwards and forwards but also from side to side. Occasionally one will find on dolls of this century walking mechanisms which are worked on a counter balance system and that the eyes are linked to the system. As the doll's legs 'walk' so the eyes move from side to side. One such example is the Roddy doll in Plate 130. It has a hard vinyl head and the body stands 21ins. tall. This doll was made by Bluebell Dolls Ltd. of Southport, England, between 1955 and 1963.

Most makers found, however, that if one required eyes to glance to the side, it was better to simply place the sleeping mechanism in the head with the glass eyes in such a position that they always glanced to the side.

Another improvement was purely cosmetic. The sleeping eye, regardless of its material, normally had the lid as an integral part. It was simple to attach the strip of upper lash to the lid and when the eye closed the strip of upper lash dropped too. Many makers continued painting on the eyelashes to the surface of the head and many dolls appear to have two sets of upper lashes when their eyes are closed. If a wax lid was used the lashes were placed between the wax and the glass of the eye. If a metal lid was used, there was a slot in the lid to take the lashes. The same method was employed when the eye was of plastic but sometimes the eye, lid and lashes were moulded as one unit.

Making eyes of glass was the most popular method and certainly they have withstood the test of time for, unless an accident has occurred, the eyes remain intact. This cannot be said for eyes made of other materials, noticeably metal or tin eyes such as those used on early Shirley Temple dolls. These eyes were enamelled with colours and over the years the enamel in many cases has crazed.

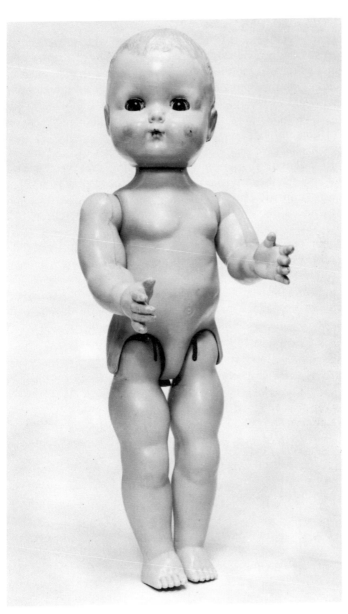

*Plate 130*

# The Mouth

Another important facial feature is the mouth and an overall picture can be obtained by studying the photographs of the heads in Chapter 1. You will see the gradual changes and development of the mouth. One should remember that the makers were attempting to create a doll whose appearance was pleasing to all including the person who actually bought the doll. Therefore, most dolls have a happy, if not smiling, face and mouth.

The first change which you will notice comes when the lips are cast into a definite shape sometimes including the central hollow running between the nose and upper lip. A second change which is even more dramatic came when the mouth was opened. This was done to create a more natural look but as a result the happy face changed into a smiling face. Usually the upper teeth only were shown and sometimes the tongue. The teeth of the majority of dolls were formed by a small, thin block of white bisque moulded into shape to represent either two or four teeth. This block was pasted to the inside of the head behind the upper lip. Occasionally a lower set of teeth was added but dolls with these often appear to be grimacing rather than smiling. Plate 131 shows the double set of teeth of a walking doll by Jules Nicholas Steiner.

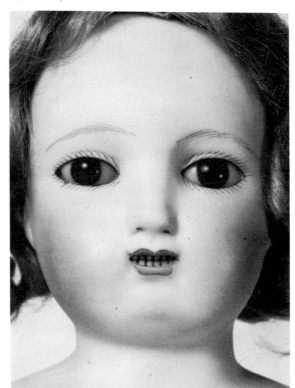

*Plate 131*

On later heads, particularly those made of stoneware, celluloid and vinyl, the teeth are sometimes found to be cast with the head. Their appearance is not as realistic, mainly because the paintwork of the teeth was not well done.

Guidelines for the mouth are given below.

1. **Wooden Dolls.** Their mouth shape deteriorated from well shaped and painted (Frontispiece, right) with long lines cut horizontally to an archer's bow shape with a short line cut to separate the lips. Later the cut lines were replaced with a painted red line with the bow shape at the centre (Frontispiece, left). Finally very late wooden heads had a simple crescent of red or even a dot.

2. **Wax over Composition Dolls.** Although moulded to shape, these mouths followed the idea of a wide horizontal line with a box shape in the middle (Plate 13, p. 28). Composition heads tended to be painted in the same manner as wooden ones, but very occasionally one might find an open mouth with teeth made of bamboo.

3. **Wax Dolls.** Normally with closed mouths, these have what might be considered a more natural mouth, not extending quite so much to each side. There are some which have open mouths and others which appear to be open slightly showing their tongues but without an actual slit or gap between the lips.

4. **Glazed China and Bisque Dolls.** The majority of these dolls appear to have rather tight mouths with well defined bows on the top lip. However, on closer examination this is formed by the paintwork of the lips rather than the casting which might give a much wider and more generous mouth. The paintwork does contribute a great deal to the character of a doll and as this part of its manufacture was individual, no two dolls are really exactly alike.

5. **Open Mouthed Dolls.** If you look at Plate 15 (p. 30), you will see a good example of the general open mouthed head with four teeth. If, however, you look at Plate 120 (p. 152), you will see the illusion of an open mouth without any hole or gap in the bisque head. This is one of the most happy and carefree looking baby dolls ever created and the effect is much more difficult to achieve than the sleeping infant look.

## The Nose

Every doll's face has a nose. It may be a single line drawn down the face, a painted knob, or a triangular wedge, or as in the case of

***Colour Plate 9.***
*Bisque socket head,
with a jointed com-
position body, glass
eyes, and a moahir
wig. Made by
Jumeau. French,
c.1885, height 20ins.*

most dolls, a properly formed nose. The shape of the nose seems to depend largely on the material used to make the head, but always the maker has tried to create an attractive nose to keep the face as a whole a pleasing object to look at. It is usually only with a character face that the nose may be changed in shape to enhance the overall look of the head.

Plate 132 shows a male socket head made of bisque mounted on a jointed composition body. This is quite a rare example of a character head as it represents not only a man but also an old man with grey eyebrows and wrinkles. Although this doll is dressed as a farmer, it is similar to those dressed as the American 'Uncle Sam'.

The nose used for most wooden dolls is a wooden triangular wedge inserted into a slit in the centre of the face before the paint-work is done. Sometimes this wedge is neatly carved to show the nostrils but in the majority of cases, it is a simple triangle. The wooden face in Plate 133 shows the slit into which the wedge would be placed.

*Plate 132*

*Plate 133*

Heads of composition and wax over composition had noses which were moulded at the same time as the rest of the head. These noses tend to be rather round and button like. Most of the poured wax heads have this type of nose. However, depending upon the degree of skill of the craftsman and the purpose of the doll the noses could be well defined and shaped with nostrils. It was equally possible to do a long aquiline nose as it was to do a button nose but the latter was and still is a more popular look. Please look at the illustration of Lord Roberts (Plate 163, p. 194) and compare it with the normal poured wax doll.

Many wax dolls have noses which have been 'blunted' through general wear and tear and being rubbed. The wax coat on wax over composition heads may at the nose area be rubbed through to the base material.

When one of the harder substances was used, such as glazed china, bisque or celluloid, it was possible to create any shape of nose desired. However, again, because they were popular, the small slightly turned-up nose was the most favoured. Vinyl dolls of today also tend to have this type of nose.

## The Ears

Not the most necessary of the facial features, but certainly an enhancement to the overall appearance, are the ears. They were only placed on the heads when they would be seen or served a purpose and while the majority of dolls do have ears, many do not, for example those with moulded hair styles which cover the ears.

The profile of the 1700 doll (Frontispiece, right) has a rather natural looking ear (Plate 134).

The profile of the 1748 doll also has rather delicate ears (Plate 135), although they are somewhat stylised in appearance. This illustration also shows the tacks used to hold the wig in place. On the other hand if you look at Plate 144 (p. 176) of Sophie, she has no ears, in fact it appears that her ears have been replaced with tacks.

Ears on moulded heads are cast as part of the face rather than as part of the back of the head and the seam usually runs along the broad back curve of the ears.

Plate 136 (p. 168) shows the profile of the doll illustrated in Plate 116 (p. 143), showing the ear. The lobe has also been pierced to hold an earring. Thought at one time to be only on French dolls,

*Plate 134*

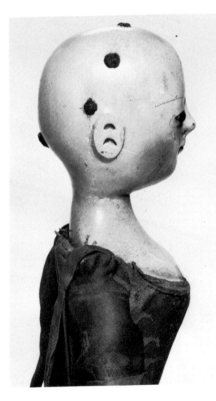

*Plate 135*

the pierced lobe is also found on many German doll heads except those representing babies.

When the heads are made of cloth, the ears can be sewn on as separate units. The profile of the Lenci doll (Plate 137, overleaf) shows the ears are of moulded felt and they have been sewn on with very fine stitches.

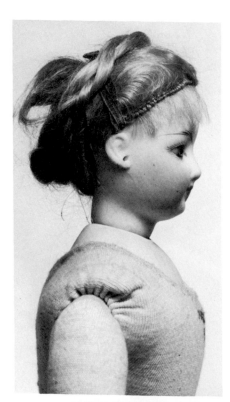

*Plate 136*

*Plate 137*

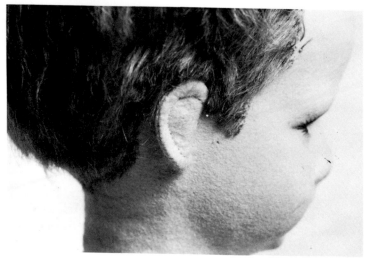

168

# Face Masks

Before leaving this chapter on facial features, there is one set of faces which some might feel should more properly be discussed in Chapter 1; these are the sewn-on faces or masks. We have already discussed sewn-on heads.

Face masks can be of composition, stiffened cloth and on rare occasions, wax. Generally they are oval in shape with some attempt at moulding the facial features and characteristics such as the eyes, nose and mouth, and appropriately painted in colours. After moulding and painting the face mask is then sewn onto a cloth head with fine stitching around the circumference of the mask. Sometimes you will find one which has been glued into place but this method has the disadvantage of the glue drying and cracking with the result that the mask may become detached.

*Plate 138*

It was possible, as it is now, to purchase a commercially produced face mask to be used on a doll which was hand made or made at home from a pattern.

Plate 138 (p. 169) shows a dolls' house doll of 1673 with a wax face attached to a linen bound head. The facial features have been painted onto a plain disc shape.

*Plate 139*

*Plate 140*

Plate 139 shows a stiffened cloth face mask which has been moulded and painted and Plate 140 shows the same doll full length. The body is soft, made of light green velvet and designed to represent a skater. This doll, although unmarked, was probably made during the 1930s by the Chad Valley company of Birmingham.

# Chapter 6
# The Hair

An important part of a doll's appearance is its hair. Not all dolls were designed to have hair added to their heads, many had moulded styles or even simple brush strokes painted as curls onto their heads to represent the hair. The shapes of the heads were also quite important for the types and style of the hair and the way it was attached or formed.

Real hair was the most common way to produce a doll's crowning glory and it was made from a variety of different types, both human and animal. Much later on nylon was used. The two most popular materials were human hair and mohair. The origins of the first are obvious and the second was formed from the hair of the Angora goat. The advantages of human hair are that it holds its styling better, can be combed through and can be restyled; its disadvantages are cost and availability. Some hand made dolls have hair known to have been cut from the head of the doll's original owner or the maker herself. The advantages of mohair are that it is cheaper and easier to style but its disadvantages are that it is difficult to clean and if combed, begins to shred. This is because mohair is spun thread and when combed begins to unravel and separate.

Both these types of hair were woven into wigs though not always on a cloth base.

Sophie's head in Plate 141 has dark brown human hair knotted to form one long strip which is nailed to the head.

Plate 142 shows the head of the 1700 doll which has a blond mohair wig with the mohair knotted to a skull-cap of linen. It covers the whole of the head and is tied with black ribbon at the nape of the neck whereas Sophie's strip is at the front only.

Mohair, when knotted to a cotton or linen base, was arranged in either spirals or circles starting at the crown centre. The inner circles or the beginning of the spiral were knotted closely together, broadening out towards the edges.

A number of dolls found today have some very strange looking

*Plate 141*

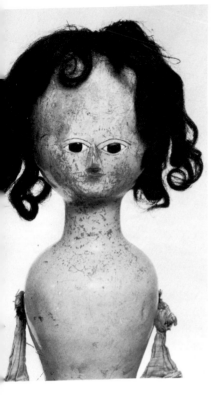

*Plate 142*

173

styles because over the years the hair has been cut and generally played with or been attacked by mice or insects. Little can be done to redress the condition and in some cases replacement wigs are necessary. These can be difficult to find and are often expensive. Many people make the mistake of using new human hair wigs, fashioned in very elaborate styles, such as ringlets, which end up looking cumbersome. Before deciding on the style needed for your doll, you should look at examples of dolls similar to your own and see what the hair styles should look like. Any new wig should be pasted to the head with a water soluble glue. Some present day glues can be very powerful and will damage the head if you try to remove them.

Other animal hair was used to form wigs, such as cowhair, but many were used only as padding for styles like chignons. Some French makers used pieces of lamb's wool complete with the skin to form the skull-caps. Easier to keep clean than most, many of these wigs now have lost their curls and simply stand up on end giving the doll a rather electrified appearance.

Modern hair for mass-produced dolls is of nylon, called in America 'saran'. It makes an ideal type for children to play with as it will withstand most washing and combing. This hair is usually inserted through small holes into the head and then knotted, a procedure called 'rooted'. Nylon hair can be made into wigs and the skull-cap base is normally of soft vinyl.

Many people have difficulty in distinguishing between the different types of hair. Human hair feels quite coarse when used on dolls and it is usually brown in colour. Mohair on the other hand is very soft, even when dirty, and slightly woolly in appearance. It may be of any colour but the predominant colour is blond. Good quality nylon hair can be quite human like but it is generally much richer in colour and very shiny.

## The Shape of the Head

A good number of dolls, particularly wooden ones, have smooth, round heads similar to the proverbial 'billiard ball', at the top. The simplest way of showing the hair is to paint the head, either with a solid colour, usually black, or to use a few well placed brush strokes.

If you look at Plate 24 (p. 41), you will see that the hair style is indicated by a block of colour which is slightly shaped at the front. No attempt has been made to carve the head. Likewise on the wax head representing Queen Victoria as a girl (Plate 162, p. 194), the head has been painted black although the wax has been shaped at the back to represent a bun. Many baby dolls have only small brush strokes to indicate their hair and possibly the best example is that of the Motschmann type where only a few curly lines do the work of a full thatch of hair. These can be seen in the profile of the Motschmann doll shown in Plate 143.

17th and 18th century dolls of wood had wigs and these were normally nailed to the heads with fairly large headed tacks. The disadvantage of this process is that the tacks have rusted and damaged the wigs, often eating away the cloth base so that the wigs fall off. These tacks also damage the paintwork of the heads, allowing cracks to form. On many wax over composition doll heads, tacks were used to attach the wigs and similar damage occurred with tacks making cracks in the wax. It is not advisable to remove the tacks unless they are already loose as this will cause even more damage.

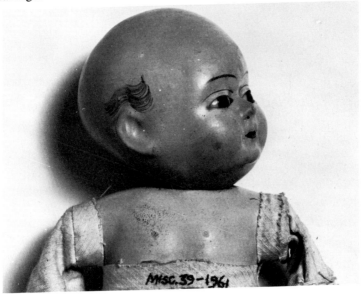

*Plate 143*

*Plate 144*

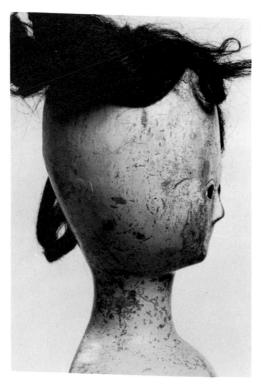

In the profile of Sophie in Plate 144 one of the tacks in the head can be seen. In fact in her case it appears this tack has replaced the ear. (See also Plate 135, p. 167, of the hairless 1748 doll.) These tacks are very rusty and have eaten through the linen base of the skullcap so that the wig now falls off.

Wigs were in common use on bisque heads but rarer on glazed china heads. Often now termed 'bald heads', glazed china heads prepared for wigs had solid crowns onto which a wig was glued. The heads were smooth and round and sometimes painted black. Other, but much rarer, methods of attaching the wigs to these heads were the use of a small hole at the crown or a slit in the top of the head. When the hole method was used a clump of hair was pasted into the hole. The slit method had a slit running from front to back across the crown into which was pasted a knotted line of hair. These methods appeared also on composition heads and wax over composition ones. Bisque heads could have any of these methods of fixing the hair but the commonest method was quite different.

As the bisque heads developed to take moving eyes and open mouths and more complex jointing, it was necessary to have easy access to the inside of the head. This was accomplished by cutting the top of the crown away. The head finished with a high forehead but low at the nape with the top edge turned inwards to form a ledge.

Plate 145 shows the top and inside view of the head to the doll shown in Plate 132 (p. 165). You can see that it is higher at the front than at the nape and also the well defined ledge. It is also possible to see the block of plaster which is used to hold the eyes in place. The two metal pieces either side of the head are additional supports sometimes used for the jointing.

*Plate 145*

When all the work on the head had been completed and it had been placed on a body, the final preparation for the wig was done. The hole in the crown was covered by a pate made of either cork or papier mâché. It was slightly rounded to follow the line of the head and to give a firm base for the wig which covered the pate entirely.

One or other of these methods was used for placing the wigs on composition, wax over composition and celluloid heads, although sometimes the wigs were just glued into place. Poured wax heads had quite different methods of attaching the hair, which was actually inserted into the wax.

The best known methods used small clumps of hair, perhaps between three and six hairs in a clump, which were inserted in rows starting at the crown. Adjustments were made if partings were required. The first method, known as the 'hot needle' process, had small holes made in the wax into which the hairs were placed. This was the method favoured by the Pierotti family. The second method, known as the 'knife cut' and favoured by the Montanari's, had small slits made in the wax into which the hairs were placed. This is the easiest method to recognise as the edges of the slits tend to show if you lift the hair up.

Many cloth dolls would have their hair sewn directly to the head. Again the hair was knotted in lines starting at the crown and shaped to form a particular style. The Lenci dolls shown in Colour Plate 10 (p. 181) have sewn-on hair.

## Moulded and Carved Hair Styles

A different treatment of the head, designed to represent the hair without using real hair, is to carve or mould the hair style. This treatment may be quite modest, for example the bun shape of the head in Plate 162 (p. 194), or very elaborate indicating the curls of the hair and even ornaments decorating the hair. The hair style of the wooden head shown in Plate 11 (p. 26) is that of a child. The head has been carved with broad, deep cuts to show a fringe with rows of tight curls.

When a head was moulded, it became much easier to produce elaborate styles. During the first part of the 19th century when lady dolls were still the most popular, many of the heads were made with very distinctive hair styles. Although the style is a good method of dating a doll, it must be remembered that, if the doll was a popular model, it may have continued in production for several years.

The composition head in Plate 146 has hair styled with large puffs at each side, a coiled plait on the crown and the back held in place by a large comb. The head is German, about 1828-30, and 3ins. high.

*Plate 146*

Plate 147 (overleaf) illustrates the back view of the glazed china heads shown in Colour Plate 1 (p. 19) showing curls, plaits and combs.

During these years, dark hair was the most fashionable but gradually lighter hair was also admired and by the 1870s and 1880s blond headed dolls were common.

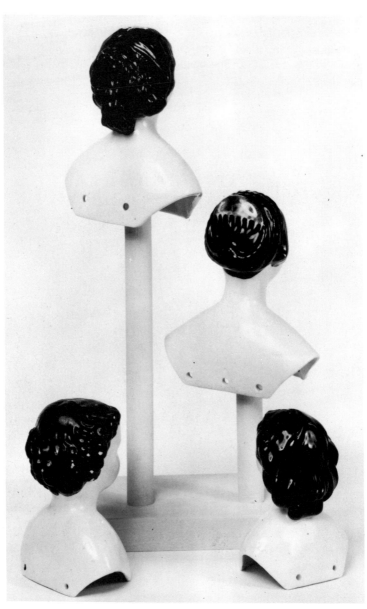

*Plate 147*

***Colour Plate 10.*** *Pair of Lenci dolls, with felt hands and bodies, painted facial features and mohair sewn to the heads. Italian, c.1927.*

*Plate 148*

*Plate 149*

The glazed china head in Plate 148 has blond hair styled in large curls which come quite low on the forehead. This is the head of the doll shown in Plate 27 (p. 48).

Moulded hair can also be found on bisque heads, chiefly on dolls representing babies. Sometimes it is a mere curl on the top, as that of the Kewpie (Plate 4, p. 18), or quite a full head of hair, as that of the Heubach character baby doll shown in Plate 50 (p. 74).

Plate 149 shows the back view of the head in Plate 17 (p. 31) showing the elaborate plaited hair style achieved on a moulded head. Note the moulded design of the chemise top along the edge of the shoulder plate and the two holes used for sewing the head to the cloth body.

Moulded hair styles reached their most elaborate with the introduction of the 'bonnet head' doll. The heads went beyond the hair styles to include bonnets, snoods and other ornamental decorations.

Plate 150 shows a bisque bonnet head with painted facial features. The hair is moulded and painted to show blond hair covered with a snood which is indicated by green criss-cross lines. The front crest is trimmed with lustre and appears to consist of a white and silver feature, a pink twist of velvet and ending in a knob of white and gold. The doll is German, made about 1868.

*Plate 150*

# Chapter 7
# Marks

Not all dolls are marked with any form of indication as to who may have been the maker or even when or where the doll was made. It is always of assistance to have a mark but it can only be used as a guideline for dating. The is no great mystery about where the marks are placed on a doll; this depends largely on the material of the doll and the whim of the maker.

Some makers used a combination of letters, names and numbers which can be quite baffling. Having sorted these, it is necessary to consult a good reference book to decipher the 'code'. It is not always possible to find details of a particular mark. Occasionally the maker merely used numbers without relating them to anything else or without recording them officially in government records by applying for a patent for example or by registering the design. Sometimes one will find a full set of marks which might be expected to identify the maker. However, records of many makers' marks do not exist. In such cases, either the maker did not register the mark officially or all records of him have been destroyed. The makers whose records appear to be missing are those whose working lives survived only a short period of time.

Plate 151 shows one of the marks used by the firm of Armand Marseille and is used to illustrate the various components of a mark. It states the doll's place of origin and the maker's name together with the maker's initials 'A M'. The number 390 is the batch or style number of the head, and the number between the initials is the size number, though it is not a reflection of the actual size, for example 9 does not indicate a 9 inch head. When the body components were added to the head, the compiler used size 9 limbs and a size 9 torso.

There are occasions when additional letters appear in the mark which indicate that the mark and/or the head design were officially recorded. The most common additions found are the following:

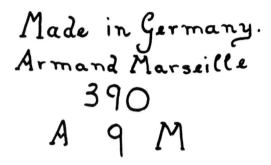

*Made in Germany.*
*Armand Marseille*
*390*
*A 9 M*

**Plate 151**

DEP — abbreviation for Deposé (French) and Deponirt (and Deponiert) (German), meaning the maker claims registration.

BREVITE or Bte — (French), meaning patented.

SGDG — abbreviation for Sans Garantie du Gouvernement (French), meaning without government guarantee.

DRGM — abbreviation for Deutsches Reichs Gebrauchs Muster (German), meaning registered design or patent.

Ges. Gesch. — abbreviation for Gesetzlich Geschutzt (German), meaning registered or patented.

Schultz Marke (German) or Trademark — the term given for the maker's own mark which could be registered.

PAT and PATd., meaning patent or patented (British and American).

Copyright, Copyr. and C together with the date and full name of the copyright owner.

The laws governing the patents, copyrights and registrations are complex and many makers seemed to be in some confusion as to which they actually held.

Heads were sometimes commissioned by other doll companies or distributors, as in the case of celluloid dolls. In such cases, it is usual to find both the maker's mark and that of the other company; however, sometimes only the commissioner's mark appears.

## Head Marks

Head marks were used exclusively on moulded heads, but it is rare to find them on early composition and glazed china heads. If you find them on a wax head, you should be very wary as it is easy to scratch on the surface of the wax at any time. It is known that some makers, both of wax and glazed china, did mark the inside of their heads. If the head is still attached to the body, then the decision must be taken whether to disturb the original stitches or loosen a very solid glue seal in order to find the mark.

Plate 152 shows moulded marks on a shoulder head. The mark is to be found generally on the shoulder plate but not always at the back. They can be at the front or on the crest of either shoulder.

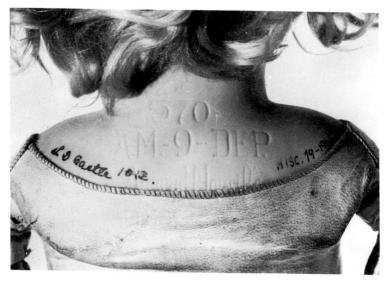

*Plate 152*

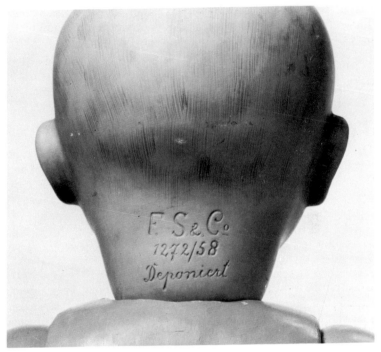

*Plate 153*

They are often covered by the material of the body. Shoulder marks can be difficult to attribute as some are just letters or numbers. This particular mark is on the doll by Armand Marseille shown in Plate 15 (p. 30) . It seems that this maker used batch numbers ending in 70 to indicate his shoulder heads and these heads related to his socket heads, for example 370 and 390 had the same faces but the first was a shoulder head and the second a socket head.

Moulded marks on socket heads were placed at the nape of the head and often covered by the hair if a wig was worn. This became the most common place to put marks and was used on dolls after 1880.

Plate 153 shows the back view of the doll shown in Plate 70 (p. 96), which was made by Franz Schmidt after 1913. You can also see the brush strokes used to indicate the hair.

Head stamps were used almost exclusively by the French firm 'Jumeau'. They were printed marks in thick red or blue paint. The one shown in Plate 154 is from a Jumeau doll made about 1885.

DEPOSE
TETE JUMEAU
Bᵗᵉ SGDG
9

*Plate 154*

## Body Stamps

Body stamps will be found usually on the front torso. They are ink stamps and often applied by the retailer rather than the maker. Such stamps are seen on cloth or kid bodies coupled with wax heads and occasionally on composition bodies.

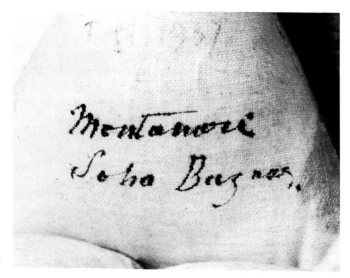

*Plate 155*

FROM E.MOODY
SOHO BAZAAR
CHAS. MARSH
SOLE MANUFACTURER
LONDON
DOLLS CLEANED & REPAIRED

Plate 156

CHAS. MARSH
SOLE MANUFACTURER
LONDON. W
DOLLS & C. REPAIRED

Plate 155 shows the Montanari mark on the torso of the doll in Plate 26 (p. 44). The doll was said to represent Princess Louise, a daughter of Queen Victoria, and it was bought at the Dublin International Exhibition of 1853 by a member of the Royal Family. The doll remained in the Royal collection until presented in 1937 to the museum by Queen Mary.

Charles Marsh marks are illustrated in Plate 156. The family of Marsh, of which Charles was a member, was listed at various London addresses from 1865 to 1913 as makers of wax and wax over composition dolls. Some of his marks included the words "Warranted to stand any climate". At the time, many families travelled to live in India and the dolls were designed to withstand the climate there which could produce some harmful effects on wax dolls. Charles Marsh also used marks which indicated that he had Royal Patronage.

Plate 157

Plate 158

Plate 159

Plate 157 shows Mrs. Lucy Peck's mark. Mrs. Peck is listed as a doll maker and repairer in London between 1891 and 1921.

Plate 158 illustrates Hamley's of London mark. This retail outlet, founded by the Hamley brothers in the mid-19th century, is still the foremost toy shop in Great Britain. The stamp is found on many wax dolls which were probably made by the Pierotti family.

The Jumeau body mark which is on the back of the torso is illustrated in Plate 159.

*Plate 160*

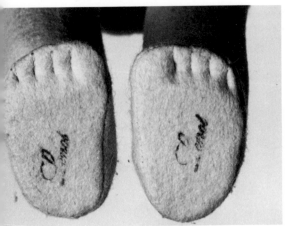

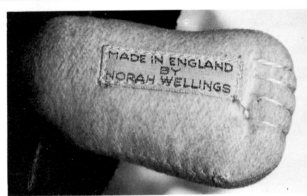

*Plate 161*

## Limb Marks

Some makers, particularly of cloth dolls, marked a limb rather than the head or body. Such marks could be signatures or stamps, as in the case of Kathe Kruse, or a cloth label sewn on, as in the case of Norah Wellings. Limb marks, whether stamped or a label, were placed on the sole of one foot.

Plate 160 shows the stamp on the sole of the foot of the Lenci doll in Plate 37 (p. 59). Plate 161 shows a Norah Wellings cloth label.

Makers of composition and bisque limbs occasionally did mark them with the size numbers which usually appear at the top or joint area of the limb.

# Labels

Labels attached to dolls served two purposes. The first purpose was to replace the maker's marks, for example the Shirley Temple doll has no marks but has a button pinned to her dress. Likewise the modern Sasha doll has a cardboard label hanging from one of its wrists. Of course, labels could be used in conjunction with the marks. The second purpose was to add information about the maker and in many cases when a maker won a prize at an exhibition for a particular doll he would add a label which stated this point.

# Chapter 8
## Character Dolls

There are several different types of dolls which can claim to be 'character' dolls. The first are those which are given names by their owners such as Sophie shown in the Frontispiece. As most dolls become imaginary friends, most children gave them a name and the name may be that of a friend, a favourite relative or of a well-known person. The name may even be that by which the owner would liked to have been known.

A second category of name is that taken to represent a person, real or imaginary, where the doll actually is dressed to be that person. With this type of character doll, there is no attempt to produce a look-alike but by using a distinctive characteristic, such as the hair style or dress, the image is created.

The doll said to represent Queen Victoria at about the age of 15 is shown in Plate 162. It has a solid wax head, wax limbs, a stuffed cloth body and glass bead eyes. The hair has been painted onto the wax but the wax at the back of the head has been modelled into a bun. This doll does not actually look very much like Queen Victoria but it has been made to represent her by the use of a particular hair style. The doll itself stands only 8½ins. tall.

Portrait dolls are another category of character dolls. It was possible to have a portrait doll made of oneself in much the same way as a painting. However, the portrait dolls which have survived tend to be of well known people. Regardless of when they lived these people were the trendsetters, be they royalty or film stars, and to this day, they form the basis for a distinct group of dolls.

A doll representing Queen Victoria is shown in Colour Plate 11 (p. 200) in which she is thought to be dressed in either her coronation robes or her robes for her first State Opening of Parliament. The doll has a poured wax head and limbs, a stuffed cloth body and glass eyes. She stands 24ins. tall.

Plate 163 shows a doll of Lord Roberts, dressed as a field marshall. The doll has a poured wax head and limbs, a stuffed

*Plate 162*

*Plate 163*

cloth body, glass eyes and grey human hair inserted into the wax. He stands 18ins. tall. The doll was probably made by a member of the Pierotti family about 1900 and the maker had previously made a similar portrait head of Lord Roberts when he was a general.

A doll representing the Tudor Princess Elizabeth, later Elizabeth I, is shown in Colour Plate 12 (p. 209). The doll has a poured wax head and limbs, a body of muslin which is made with a wire framework and stuffed with polyester fibre, glass eyes and human hair inserted into the wax. The doll stands 17ins. tall.

The doll was designed for and given to the Bethnal Green Museum of Childhood in 1977 by the maker, Sheila Wallace. Sheila, a well known American craftswoman who follows in the line of traditional wax modellers, stated that she thought that Princess Elizabeth had the same sort of doubts and problems experienced by all young people and tried to show on the doll the idea of a girl with a turbulent, if unknown, future.

Wax was and still is the easiest of the materials with which to work when creating a portrait doll. It must be also remembered that most wax doll makers called themselves Wax Modellers which suggests that they did not see themselves as merely the makers of playthings. Composition and plastics have also been used, but rarely glazed china or bisque.

A doll representing Herbert Horatio, Earl Kitchener of Khartoum, is shown in Plate 164. The doll has a composition head, composition hands and feet, with a stuffed cloth body, painted facial features and intaglio eyes. The hair has been carefully moulded and the feet modelled and painted to represent boots. The doll stands 19ins. tall.

*Plate 164*

195

During the First World War, German dolls were not imported. To replace the dolls, many firms and volunteer organisations were formed to provide toys for children, amongst them the Lord Robert's Memorial Workshops for Disabled Soldiers and Seamen. National heroes of the day were popular characters to portray and Lord Kitchener was one of a set produced in 1915 which included King George V, Albert, King of the Belgians, and Lord Jellicoe.

Colour Plate 13 (p. 212), shows the Shirley Temple doll has a composition head and body, with greenish enamelled tin eyes and a mohair wig. Pinned to her dress is a button showing a photograph of Shirley Temple, the American child star, who was at the height of her film career between 1934 and 1939. The doll was made by the Ideal Toy and Novelty Company and stands 22ins. tall. Morris Michtom, famous for his introduction of the teddy bear, founded the company in 1907 in New York. The company is now known as the Ideal Toy Corporation and over the years has designed and produced a wide range of dolls and toys. It has occasionally re-issued the Shirley Temple doll since 1939 though modern versions are made of vinyl.

The final category of character dolls are those which were named, not by their owners, but by their makers. There had been a gradual attempt to create a more lifelike and natural doll which reflected not just the pretty face but all the different expressions of children. To this end, a number of makers vied with each other to produce 'Character Heads'. The most prominent, at the time, was the firm of Kammer and Reinhardt which introduced in 1909 a series starting with the mould number 100. This number, which represented a young baby, sometimes called the Kaiser Baby, was supposed to be a smiling, happy face but as the dolls were individually painted, their facial expressions could appear to be anything between the happy face and that of a screaming child. An example is shown in Plate 165. The doll has a bisque socket head, with a bent limb composition body, intaglio eyes and moulded hair. It is 11ins. tall.

Plate 166 shows Elsie, mould number 109, registered in 1910. The doll has a bisque socket head, ball jointed composition body, intaglio eyes and a mohair wig. It is 22ins. tall. This model by Kammer and Reinhardt became the least popular of all the character heads the company produced. This was probably due to its rather sad and pensive expression.

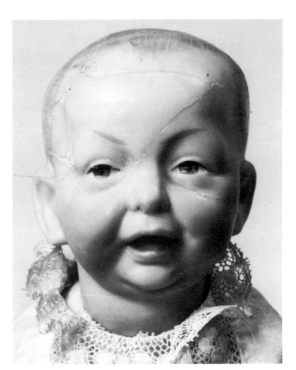

*Plate 165*

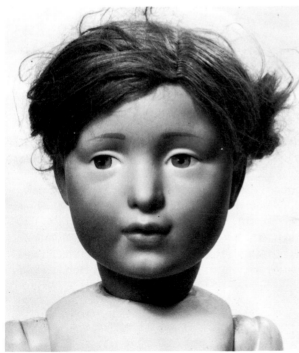

*Plate 166*

197

Other makers were quick to follow suit and the firm of Gebruder Heubach produced some very fine examples.

The baby in Plate 167 with a bisque socket head has a bent limb composition body, intaglio eyes and moulded hair. It was made about 1910 and stands 15ins. tall.

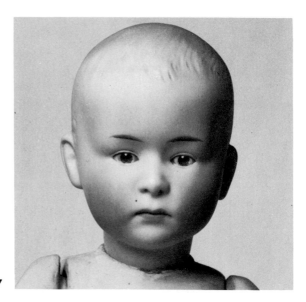

*Plate 167*

Many German companies did not survive the Second World War but there are two major designers of character heads and dolls whose work has survived to the present time although the dolls are now made of vinyl.

The doll shown in Plates 35 and 36 (p. 58) was made by Kathe Kruse, the wife of the sculptor Max Kruse. Due to his insistence not to give mass-produced dolls to his children, Kathe created a new, unbreakable and washable series of dolls individually modelled on children which she sketched. The dolls usually had a realism not captured by the ordinary character face. Kathe Kruse began manufacturing what she called artistic dolls in 1910 and continued until her death in 1968. Production still continues today at Donauworth in Germany.

*Plate 168*

*Plate 169*

**Colour Plate 11.** *Portrait doll, representing Queen Victoria. The wax shoulder head, with glass eyes and a human hair wig, is mounted on a cloth body. English, c.1840, height 24ins.*

Another series of character dolls was designed by a Swiss artist called Sasha Morgenthaler. She began to create this type of doll in the 1940s and she had a "vision of how a child would look and move in the age of innocence". The early dolls were expensive and generally beyond the reach of most children. Her dream that these special creations could be available to every child, not just a privileged few, came true when Sasha met John and Sarah Doggart who owned Trendon Toys and were at the time looking for a doll design which was more meaningful than the standard doll.

Plate 168 (p. 199) shows a 'Brunnette' Sasha doll of moulded plastic with painted facial features and rooted nylon hair. The doll was made by Trendon Toys Ltd. in 1970, and she stands 16ins. tall.

Even to the present day, makers produced named dolls, for example the Sindy Doll. Not all them however prove to be popular.

Kelly, an all vinyl doll which is jointed at the neck, shoulders, waist, and hips and has knee joints beneath the outer vinyl, is shown in Plate 169 (p. 199). The doll was launched in October 1979 by Marks and Spencer Ltd., and was made by Pedigree. It was designed to represent an 18 year old girl. Unfortunately the popularity of the doll did not reach expectations and it was withdrawn from sale.

Some present day makers are working with the traditional materials. One of these is Margaret Glover of London, who works with wax and creates known characters such as Christopher Robin. Other makers create their own character dolls which are based on ideals rather than known characters.

In Plate 170 we see Willie Wistful, with a bisque shoulder head and limbs, and a cloth body. It has a character face and represents 'the All American Boy', a Huckleberry Finn type character. To add to this image the doll carries a slingshot and goes bare footed. This doll was designed by Martha Martin in February 1979 and made by her husband, Bill, under the copyright Wistful Dolls. Plate 171 illustrates the head of Willie Wistful, showing the signature of the designer.

Margaret Glover and Bill and Martha Martin are individual craftsmen. There are several manufacturers who produce known character dolls, usually with vinyl but occasionally of more traditional materials.

*Plate 170*

*Plate 171*

*Plate 172*

Plate 172 shows Queen Victoria, no. 13 of a limited edition of 500 which were produced by Tower Treasures Ltd. and designed by Peggy Nisbet in 1976. This doll has a bisque head and limbs with a kid body. The doll is fashioned after the portrait by H. Von Angeli of Queen Victoria, done in 1899. Peggy Nisbet's firm produces not only these rather expensive high quality dolls but also a range of good quality but reasonably priced character dolls of vinyl. Her range covers two types, those with individually designed heads, for example one of Winston Churchill, and those with stylised heads which are dressed to represent a type of person or style of clothing, for example the Harrods Doorman.

Character dolls are great fun to collect as they appear to have just that little bit more expression and individuality. Whether the doll has a happy, sad or even crying or sleeping face, by having just one character doll, your collection will be just a little more exciting.

An unusual extension of the character doll are those dolls which have more than one face. Commonly called multi-faced, these dolls will have either a head with a happy face on one side and a sad, crying or sleeping face on the other, or the head will be designed to show three faces — happy, sad or crying, and sleeping. An example is shown in Plates 173-175. The head is bisque, with a cardboard body which contains a sound mechanism, wooden limbs, cloth upper legs and glass eyes. A few strands of hair are attached to each face and the head is contained within a cardboard hood which extends to form the shoulder plate. Note the tear drop in the crying face (Plate 174).

From the mid-1860s, quite a number of patents were taken out for multi-faced heads and perhaps the two two major makers were Fritz Bartenstein and Carl Bergner, both of Germany. Both wax over composition and bisque were used to make the heads and, occasionally, you will find a contemporary vinyl doll of this type.

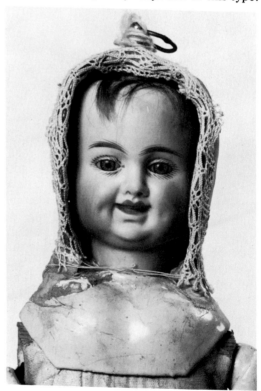

*Plate 173*

*Plate 174*

*Plate 175*

In Chapter 7, p. 187, I mentioned the fact that the firm of Armand Marseille would use the same face style for both shoulder and socket heads. This firm also produced similar heads and faces with slight changes made to the facial expression, and it is probable that it was the only firm to do so. The most noticible example is the set of dolls called My Dream Baby which bear the batch numbers 341 or 351. This doll, representing a young baby, was designed to have either a closed mouth (no. 341) or an open mouth (no. 351) which sometimes showed two teeth.

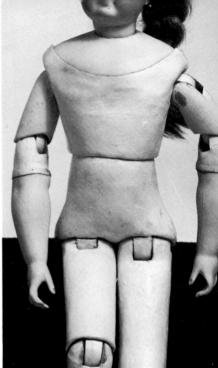

*Plate 176*

*Plate 177*

# The Rare and Unusual Dolls

There are many different types of dolls and the majority fall within the guidelines already set out. Nevertheless there are a few doll types which, because of the inventiveness of their creators, have very distinct characteristics. It would seem that the changes in the characteristics of mass-produced dolls throughout the period occurred not only because of the introduction of new materials and methods, but also because the makers continually strove to create a more human like figure. If you look at Plate 112 (p. 137), the Charles Motschmann doll, you will see one of the most radical attempts at creating a new jointing system.

More normal to look at, but equally unusual when compared to other French kid bodies of the same date, is the fully jointed kid body of about 1870. With this example, the swivel head and lower arms are of bisque while the rest of the body and the limbs are of kid stretched over a wood and composition frame. The doll is jointed at the shoulders, elbows, waist, hips, knees and ankles and these joints are held in place with metal pins rather than elastic. This method of jointing is similar to a number of patents taken out in the 1860s including one by Leon Casimir Bru for a cardboard body in 1869.

Plate 176 (p. 206) shows a swivel head and upper chest. Plate 177 (p. 206) shows the jointed arms and body with a waist joint. The shoulder joints move in a circular swivel as well as outwards. Plate 178 shows a front view of the hips and legs, and Plate 179 the back view of the hips and legs. This illustration also shows the almost smooth line of the seam of the kid covering.

This doll, which stands 18ins. tall, is one of a pair and was packed in a green cardboard box, with a printed blue and white label. The label reads: "No. 4703 Maquette" and shows a mark of a girl with her arms around the neck of a lamb. Unfortunately, there is no trace of the origins of this label at the present time.

Similar in appearance was a spring jointed wooden doll patented by Albert Schoenhut of Philadelphia, USA, in 1911. Called "All-Wood Perfection Art Dolls", they were jointed at the neck, shoulders, elbows, wrists, hips, knees and ankles. The jointing was

*Plate 178*                                              *Plate 179*

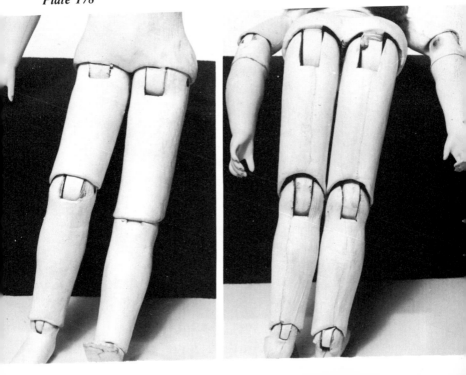

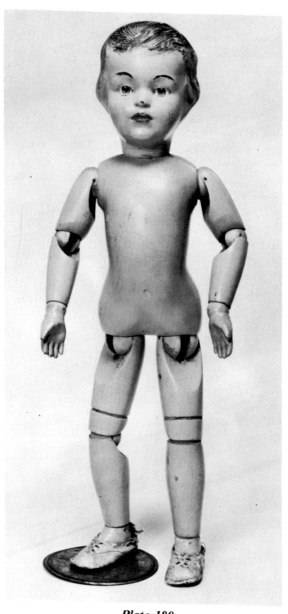

*Plate 180*

***Colour Plate 12.*** *Portrait doll, representing the Tudor Princess Elizabeth.*
*The wax headed doll was made by Sheila Wallace, USA, 1977, height 17ins.*

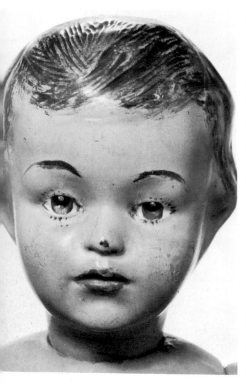

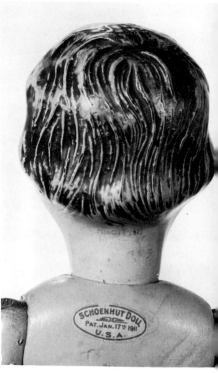

**Plate 181**

**Plate 182**

held by "patent steel spring hinges having double spring tensions and swivel connections", which were flexible but tight enough to hold any position. In the base of each foot were drilled two holes to fit onto the spike of a metal stand. One hole was straight so the foot could rest flat while the other hole was oblique to hold the foot in a tip-toe position.

Plate 180 (p. 208) shows a Schoenhut boy doll with moulded hair and intaglio eyes. He is painted with enamel colours and could be washed. He stands 16½ins. tall. The dolls were issued dressed in a white union suit or fully clothed. The manufacturers of this doll made many character heads, some with wigs, also baby dolls and a 'manikin' doll complete with a jointed waist. Plate 181 shows the head of the doll in detail. Plate 182 shows the back view of the head and upper chest, showing the moulded hair style and the mark.

*Plate 183*

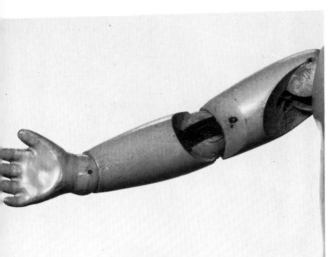

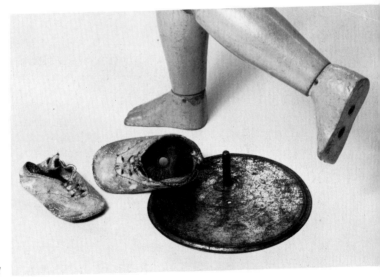

*Plate 184*

Plate 183 shows the inner side of the arm and the elbow joint, and Plate 184 the lower leg and the ankle showing the holes in the feet and the stand and shoes supplied with the dolls.

Rarely seen in England are dolls by two American makers which

*Colour Plate 13.* Portrait doll, representing Shirley Temple. The all composition jointed doll was made by the Ideal Toy and Novelty Co., USA, 1934-9, height 22ins.

are really quite unusual. In 1873, Izannah Walker patented a process for making rag dolls and their heads which used layers of cloth treated with glue and then pressed into a mould. After this moulding the forms were covered with a padding and a top layer of stockinet and then replaced in the mould for a final pressing before being painted with oils.

The second was Martha Kenks Chase who produced from the 1880s stockinet dolls including a life size model for use in a hospital. The heads of her dolls were made of stockinet stretched over a moulded base which had the necessary facial features. The stockinet was then sized before being painted with oils to give a surface which could be washed. The bodies were of cloth, sateen to start with and later cotton, stuffed with cotton wool. Her first dolls were fully jointed but by the 1920s only the shoulders and hips actually moved. She made a great many styles including babies and children, and characters from books such as *Alice in Wonderland*.

# Chapter 9
## Movement and Sound

As further attempts were made to create more natural dolls and to recreate various human abilities, makers employed a great number of ways and devices to make dolls move and produce sound.

The simplest method of making a doll move was through the use of vibrations. Bristle dolls are tiny wooden figures of turned and painted wood with freely moving legs suspended below the body. The body itself is supported by four bristles. These dolls were designed to be placed on the sound board of a musical instrument. The vibrations produced by the playing of the instrument caused the figures to appear to dance. These are shown in Plate 185. They are traditional toys from Germany, made over a period of several hundred years.

*Plate 185*

**Plate 186**

A variation of the bristle doll is the dancing doll which uses a loosely jointed figure supported by a rod in its back which is held by the operator. The doll is stood on a thin piece of wood which the operator taps in time with music and as the board vibrates the doll dances.

Plate 186 shows a Tommy Dancing doll, made by a soldier during the First World War.

Mechanical aids were used to recreate the effect too. By placing a wooden figure, usually quite small and supported by thin wire, on a cloth-covered rubber vibrating panel which is activated by batteries and a microphone to pick up sound, the figure will dance. Many different dancing dolls of these types have been made over the years, often of thin cardboard. Although they may look different, they all have loosely jointed limbs, some method of support and are called Dancing Dolls.

*Plate 187*

Plate 187 shows a pair of dancing dolls operated by a clockwork mechanism. Each doll is supported by an upright metal post which goes into the box below and attaches to one end of a bar. The clockwork mechanism makes the bar work in a see-saw movement, jostling each doll in turn. It is very quick and the dolls appear to be constantly on the move.

Another movement type is to jerk the limbs about by pulling a string. Termed 'Jumping Jacks' here and 'Pantins' in France, these figures can be of wood or cardboard, also loosely jointed. A length of string is passed from each arm and leg to hang down between the legs. When the string is pulled the arms and legs are jerked upwards and outwards. This type of doll is often now seen in plastic as crib toys for very young children.

*Plate 188*

*Plate 189*

Plate 188 shows an Arlechino (Harlequin) jumping jack of printed cardboard and Plate 189 the figure in the position when the string has been pulled. This figure was produced as a sheet to be cut out and linked together by Franz Joseph Holler of Munich in co-operation with the Museo Nationale della Arti e Tradizioni Popolari, Rome, in 1979.

217

*Plate 190*

Another young child's toy is the Tumbler or Knock-about Doll. This type of doll has a round base which is weighted and when the doll is pushed over it automatically returns to an upright position.

Tumblers, made of celluloid with a lead weight in the base, are shown in Plate 190. Perhaps this combination of materials would not be suitable today, but it is possible to get such dolls made of plastics and of cloth. They were made in Germany about 1914. This type of doll is also known as a 'Kelly' doll or 'Stehauffmanchen' doll.

While all of these dolls move, none of them actually walk. More advanced movements required more complicated mechanisms. As described with the Roddy walking doll (Plate 130, p. 161) the legs could be made to 'walk' by using a counterbalance which throws one leg in front of the other to produce a rather rolling gait. The counterbalance is like a switch being housed within the lower body but requiring no clockwork. This method has been used frequently on dolls made within the last thirty years.

It was the use of a clockwork mechanism introduced into dolls during the 1860s which transformed a stationary doll into a walking figure. Coming in several different forms, the earliest was the

*Plate 191*

Autoperipatetikos patented July 5, 1862, in America and in December of the same year in Europe, by E.R. Morrison. It is probable that these dolls were made by several people, but the majority bear the name Martin & Runyan of New York, a firm which also had offices in London. Small dolls, standing only 10ins. tall, had brass leg casings shaped like boots which lifted up, moved a step and lowered again, alternately. In practice, while the boot lifted up, neither foot actually left the ground because within each there is a curved bar and it is the bar which 'walks'. Alternately the bars come down to the ground to protrude below the boot, move on the curved edge about one quarter of an inch, then lift up into the leg again while the other foot remains firmly planted on the ground. It is a very smooth movement altogether. Plate 191 (p. 219) shows an Autoperipatetikos with a composition head, cardboard conical shaped body housing the mechanism, and kid arms. Other types of heads were used, generally glazed china.

Many walking dolls actually glided on wheels hidden by long skirts. Normally they had three wheels, a central one at the front or back for steering the doll, a drive wheel to move the doll along and a third wheel for balance. The clockwork turned the drive wheel only. In many cases the dolls had no legs but sometimes the whole doll was mounted on wheels.

*Plate 192*

Plate 192 illustrates a walking doll made by Jules Nicholas Steiner, showing the base of the doll with its three holes. To the right is the key for winding up the clockwork and the stop lever. The head of this doll is shown in Plate 131 (p. 162).

The simplest method of making sounds uses a bellows of kid or paper situated in the torso of the doll. The bellows could be operated by depressing them through the body, as in the case of the Motschmann doll, and the sound produced is a squeak. Plate 193 shows the cloth torso of the Motschmann doll housing a paper bellows.

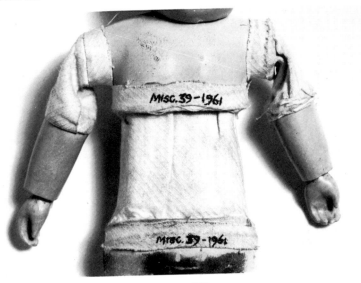

*Plate 193*

A slightly more refined method was to attach a string which protruded from the body. When the string was pulled, the bellows were depressed and the sound emitted, commonly referred to as saying 'MAMA'. Some makers had two strings and the doll would say MAMA and PAPA. Bellows could also be linked to a clockwork mechanism which operated some other movement, usually a walk.

The interior of the Steiner walking doll in Plate 194 shows the bellows and part of the clockwork mechanism. When performing

221

*Plate 194*

this doll has the distinction of looking like a Parisian fashion model gliding along while at the same time screaming 'Mama'. When this doll walks, she also moved her arms up and down in unison.

A mechanical method using an actual record was invented by Thomas Edison in 1878, though not really perfected within a realistic doll for another ten years. His dolls used a tiny wax cylinder mounted on a metal rod which protruded from the body and was operated by a key. When the key was turned, a needle resting on the cylinder produced the sound. Later developments also used a record, though its shape changed to a disc, which could be operated by clockwork. Present day talking dolls have a battery operated mechanism and the disc is activated by pulling a string which protrudes from the body.

Clockwork mechanisms were used in many different toys and dolls to create movement and sounds. It seems now that makers tried to adapt their toys for use with clockwork and anything that could move or make a sound was given the aids to do so. Perhaps one of the most fascinating is the Swimming Doll. Various patents

*Plate 195*

were obtained from the 1870s onwards in France and Germany for swimming dolls and the one shown here in Plates 195 and 196 is based on a patent taken out in 1878 by E. Martin of Paris. It is 17ins. long. The bisque socket head was made by Simon and Halbig about 1905 and it is on a cork body which houses the clockwork

### Plate 196

mechanism. The arms and jointed legs are of painted wood and the cup shaped hands of metal. The doll will swim on her back as well as her front and at one time was dressed in an oiled silk swimsuit. Although this doll will still swim in water, by clawing her way with her hands, it is so difficult to dry her out again that now she must be content to swim in air.

# Chapter 10
# Fakes

The most disastrous result of the recent upsurge of doll collecting is the unscrupulous production of fakes, deliberately produced and sold as old original dolls, to cash in on the expensive doll trade and ultimately defraud the public. Such dolls now tend to be those at the expensive end of the market, the Brus and Jumeaus and occasionally 18th century woodens, but the making of fakes is not a recent phenomenon as attested by the three aptly named 'School for Scandal' dolls in the Bethnal Green Museum's collection (Plate 197). Fakes are not dolls reproduced by modern makers using their own designs or moulds taken from original heads, carefully marked and priced so that the buying public realises that they are acquiring reproductions or modern dolls made by the traditional methods.

To the practised eye, modern fakes are usually easy to identify. There are certain guidelines which individually may mean replacement parts but collectively add up to the suggestion of a fake. Most dolls faked are made with bisque heads and the first guideline is the wig which will be new and probably made of human hair.

The second and by far the most important indication of a fake is the head. Unless a maker has been extraordinarily lucky to have found a master head, he will have made his mould from a cast taken directly from an original head. Due to the properties of porcelain, there is considerable shrinkage when firing takes place and the new head will be smaller than the original. Also, with the examples I have seen, there is a loss of quality both with the material and the colouring and imperfections occur such as very tiny pimples on the surface. Of course, I have the opportunity to compare any head I see with one with a documented history but the third guideline is often quite easy to recognise and that is the condition of the body.

Most dolls now faked have either kid or composition bodies and occasionally cloth ones. If a doll has been well cared for, kid bodies

*Plate 197*

will be immaculate with only slight scuffed or dirty patches occurring on exposed areas, such as the legs, if at all. Composition bodies may show the scuff marks at the joints and some wear on exposed areas. Badly treated dolls could have damaged bodies or very dirty bodies but they *do not* have mottled bodies. This effect is seen on fake kid and cloth bodies and appears as if the material has been stained with tea. Should you see such a body, it might well be a fake because if the body were a replacement, there would be no reason to stain it. Look also very carefully at the paintwork and if you are in any doubt about the doll seek expert advice, preferably before you buy it.

The limbs will depend upon the rest of the body and the head and they will follow the guidelines already stated. One final check to be made is the inside of the head. However well treated, an old doll always has a fine layer of dust inside its head which modern ones have not yet acquired. The difficulty of recognising present day fakes will arise in the future when they too have acquired all the trappings of age.

Plate 197 shows a fake of an 18th century wooden doll. If you compare this doll with Sophie (Frontispiece, left) (the type she is supposed to represent) the first difference is the hair which is human formed over a stiffened net base and stuck with a plaster-like substance. Although the face looks somewhat like that of a late 19th century Dutch doll, the main giveaway is the eyes which are blown glass balls set into the head instead of lozenge shaped pieces. The hands and the body are also wrong, being crudely carved but not as basic in design as either Sophie's body or the hands of the doll shown in Plate 81 (p. 106). The clothing did not add realism to the whole either, although the dress material is a late 18th century silk. The style is wrong and the decorations, comprising items of both the 19th and 20th century, include the large pearlised beads on the skirt and the green bead earrings which were common during the 1920s. This doll represents Mrs. Candour, a character in the *School for Scandal* which was first produced at the Drury Lane Theatre in May 1777. This doll, together with those of Lady Teazle and Lady Sneerwell, was exhibited at the Children Through the Ages Exhibition, Chesterfield House, London, in April and May 1934 and was classified as an 18th century doll. In fact the three dolls were made just before the 1934 exhibition. They were acquired by the Victoria and Albert Museum in 1947 as 18th century dolls and have been retained because, although they have a dubious history and are fakes, they are now really quite rare.

# Chapter 11

# Advice for the New Collector of Dolls

Dolls are fun to collect; they help to recapture your childhood and may be a somewhat unusual talking point. By collecting dolls, you will be investing pounds in tens and hundreds rather than in thousands as very few of these objects fetch more than a thousand pounds. The person with a limited budget can form a good collection of dolls which will be worthwhile yet very enjoyable.

Before deciding whether to collect dolls, one should ask this fundamental question, "Will I enjoy having these objects in my house?" Dolls are intended to represent human beings and many appear to have their own personalities, so people need to like the dolls which they collect, and feel that they would enjoy playing with and looking at them. Once this question is answered, the others such as "Where do I keep them?", "How much can I afford?" and "When do I stop?" will seem simple.

Perhaps the greatest urge to start collecting dolls is when one is found, for example, in the family attic, which may have belonged to you, your parents or even grandparents. You will probably wish to find out about its history and gradually you will form an interest in the whole range of dolls. A second starting point is when you buy at random from a sale or a shop a doll which has attracted you. Again you will probably seek out its history and thus gain your initial interest.

When people begin their collections, they tend to buy simply each and every doll they see. They also find that once the word gets out that they are collecting, their friends will start giving them dolls. As you sort out your likes and dislikes, a pattern will develop of the type of doll which you prefer.

At this stage, as your interest increases, you should acquire books on the subject, learn of museums which house the objects and possibly join clubs and attend lectures. Your initial interest will probably turn into an overwhelming passion and the dolls will rule your life and most certainly your household.

As you become more knowledgeable, your tastes may well change. You will become more selective and, rather than buying every doll available, you will choose only those which enhance your own individual collection. You may concentrate on a particular type of doll, such as only those made of wood or wax. You might decide that dolls made by one maker are more to your liking or those of a definite style, such as dolls which have moulded hair styles. The selection process will, of course, not stop your collecting any doll you like and most people only limit their collecting to a certain extent. However, it is worth mentioning that there are people who will only collect certain dolls, for example portrait dolls of known people, or those which look like someone they know, often their children.

If you decide that you are attracted to the idea of collecting dolls, the best piece of advice is to be able to distinguish between the different materials from which the heads are made. Because of the finishes given to the heads, many people have difficulty seeing whether a head is of wax, china, wood or plastic. It is always advisable to buy a doll from a reputable shop or saleroom where they have had the experience of dealing with dolls. If you acquire a doll in this way, its past history and ownership is lost; however, you can find out about where and when it was made and if there is a known maker.

If you are given a doll, ask questions about its history, who owned it, was it a gift and did it have a name. You must be cautious about some details, especially the date. Many people were given dolls by relatives as presents for their christenings, birthdays and Christmas and assume that because it was received from their grandmother, for example, she owned it as a child. This is in fact rarely the case, the grandmother bought the doll as a present and a more realistic question to ask at this point is for which birthday, etc., did you receive it.

A further consideration is the question of how much you can afford to pay for a doll. They range in cost from a few pounds to several thousands but the majority lie within the range of £50 to £750. For the new collector on a limited budget, there is the possibility of those dolls made just pre-1939 and those made between 1945 and 1960. After this date, the new soft vinyl dolls appeared and some of the models are still available. Of course, there is no reason why these should not be collected as well and they make an ideal starting set for children. Equally suitable for collecting are modern dolls made with the traditional materials and reproductions. Most modern dolls have great charm and they have a price range within most people's budget.

The most fashionable dolls to collect at the moment are the 17th and 18th century English woodens, the French bisque dolls of the 1860 to 1880 period, character dolls, and those dolls made by the two famous Parisian firms of Jumeau and Bru. As a result, the dolls in these various groups are expensive to buy.

Having acquired your first doll, the next problem is where to put it. A doll was designed to be played with and be admired, and it is not happy being placed in a dark cupboard. The best home, which allows you to enjoy the doll, is a secure glass cabinet placed out of direct sunlight and not against radiators or hot water pipes. Dolls need the same amount of care and attention that any work of art requires, and one should not be misled by the idea that a doll is merely a toy. Protection must be given against breakage, theft, light, heat and dirt.

Armed with your new interest which will quickly turn into an absorbing hobby and a delight, join a club, either one in your local area or the national one, The Doll Club of Great Britain. These clubs organise talks, visits to both museums and private collections and hold Christmas fêtes and 'bring and buy' sales. At the meetings you will have the chance to discuss and discover all sorts of dolls and meet all types of people. Every member becomes a participating member and you will have the opportunity of talking to and sharing your knowledge with others.

Collecting and thus investing in dolls does not merely mean possible financial gain; it opens an entirely new world to you, one of imagination and appreciation. Dolls show the real world in miniature and reflect the changing pattern of history. But above all, whether you are a new collector or one of many years' standing, remember that dolls were made for enjoyment.

# Bibliography

ANDERTON, J.G., *Twentieth Century Dolls from Bisque to Vinyl* (Trojan Press, 1971)

ANGIONE, G., and WHORTON, J., *All Dolls are Collectible* (Crown, 1977)

BACHMANN, M., and HAUSMANN, C., *Dolls the Wide World Over* (Harrap, 1973)

BOEHN, M. Von, *Dolls* (Dover, 1972)

BULLARD, H., *The American Doll Artist,* Vol. 1 and 2 (Summit Press, 1977)

COLEMAN, D., E., and E., *The Age of Dolls* (Coleman, 1965)
*The Collectors' Encyclopaedia of Dolls* (Crown, 1968)
*The Collectors' Encyclopaedia of Dolls' Clothes* (Crown, 1975
*Lenci Dolls* (Hobby Horse Press, 1977)

COOPER, M., and VAN KAMPEN, D., *A Taste of Honey: Googleys, Characters, Costumes* (Omni, 1976)

EARLY, A.K., *English Dolls, Effigies and Puppets* (Batsford, 1955)

EATON, F., *Dolls in Colour* (Blandford, 1975)

FOX, C., *The Doll* (Abrams, 1972)

GERKEN, J.E., *Wonderful World of Wax* (Doll Research Associates, 1964)
*Wonderful World of Papier Mâché* (Doll Research Associates, 1970)

HILLIER, M., *Dolls and Doll Makers* (Weidenfeld & Nicolson, 1968)

KING, C.E., *The Collector's History of Dolls* (Hale, 1977)
*The Price Guide to Dolls* (Antique Collectors' Club, 1977)

SMITH, P.R., *Modern Collector's Dolls,* four vols. (Collector's Books, 1973, 1975, 1976, 1979)

WALKER, F., and WHITTON, M., *Playthings by the Yard: The Story of Cloth Dolls* (Hadley, 1974)

WHITE, G., *European and American Dolls* (Batsford, 1966)

WHITTON, M., *The Jumeau Doll* (Dover, 1980)

# Museums

This list contains only public museums housing sizeable collections of dolls. There are others, both public and private and international, which are listed in the books given in the Bibliography.

BANGOR, Penrhyn Castle Museum
BATH, Museum of Costume
EDINBURGH, Museum of Childhood
LANCASTER, Museum of Childhood, Judges' Lodging
LONDON, Bethnal Green Museum of Childhood
NORWICH, Strangers' Hall Museum
WARWICK, Warwick Doll Museum
YORK, The Castle Museum

# Index

\* = main use

* = main use

* = main use

* = main use

* = main use

\* = main use

* = main use